Weeding Out The Tears

Weeding Out The Tears

A Mother's Story of Love, Loss and Renewal

Jeanne White

with Susan Dworkin

Foreword by Phil Donahue

AVON BOOKS  NEW YORK

AVON BOOKS
A division of
The Hearst Corporation
1350 Avenue of the Americas
New York, New York 10019

Copyright © 1997 by Jeanne White
Interior design by Kellan Peck
Visit our website at **http://AvonBooks.com**
ISBN: 0-380-97328-6

Library of Congress Cataloging in Publication Data:

White, Jeanne.
    Weeding out the tears : a mother's story of love, loss, and renewal / Jeanne White, with Susan Dworkin : introduction by Phil Donahue.
        p.   cm.
    1. AIDS (Disease) in children—Patients—Family relationships.
    2. White, Jeanne.   3. Mothers—Biography.   4. White, Ryan—Health.
    I. Dworkin, Susan.   II. Title.
    RJ387.A25W44   1997
    362.1'969792'0092–dc21   96-47132
    [B]   CIP

First Avon Books Printing: April 1997

AVON TRADEMARK REG. U.S. PAT. OFF. AND IN OTHER COUNTRIES, MARCA REGISTRADA, HECHO EN U.S.A.

Printed in the U.S.A.

FIRST EDITION

RRD   10   9   8   7   6   5   4   3   2   1

This book is dedicated to
my wonderful daughter,
Andrea,
my strength, my joy, my dearest friend.

Acknowledgments

For their help in the preparation of this book, thanks are due to Marcia Blacklidge, Judy Burnett, Phil Donahue, Steve Ginder, Roy Ginder, Tom and Gloria Hale, Tommy and Deb Hale, Shelley and Tom Henson, Dr. Martin Kleiman, Stuart Krichevsky, Janet and Leo Joseph, Karen Lippert, Kathy Lucas, Chris MacNeil, Michael Morrison, Tom Sheridan, Andrea White, Ryan White, Carrie Jackson Van Dyke and our editor, Ann McKay Thoroman.

—JW/SD

Who lived there?
He must have been a gardener who cared a lot,
Who weeded out the tears and grew a good crop.
And now we pray for rain,
And with every drop that pours,
We hear your name.

From "Empty Garden"
by Elton John and Bernie Taupin

Contents

Weeding Out The Tears

By Phil Donahue

"I don't know how I'm going to live without my little boy."

I had never heard Jeanne White cry, and even though I knew immediately what this call was about, the quiver in her voice shook me. I had watched her with Ryan, always physically behind him but near enough for whatever he needed, from helping him don his mod denim jacket to quickly finding a men's room where he could vomit in privacy.

Here was a woman who had taken a lot of abuse, the hostile stares in public places, the vulgarities of callers to a local radio station, even a bullet through her living room window. For five years she had watched her son die, and now that he was about to, her doctor, her family and her friends were, for the first time, going to see Jeanne White cry.

She had been all the mother Ryan White ever needed, and now, on a March Saturday morning shortly after meeting Ronald and Nancy Reagan, she was spent from a hastily reserved U.S. Air red-eye flight from Los Angeles to Indianapolis; and as she spoke into a pay phone in a hallway at Riley Hospital for Children, she was scared to death. Super Mom was finally collapsing.

"They're going to put Ryan on a respirator."

"Does Ryan know?" I asked.

"You know Ryan," she said. "He's gotta know everything."

"What did he say?"

" 'As long as there's a chance, Mom,' " she quoted him.

"Tell me what you want me to do," I said. "I'll do anything."

"I can't reach Elton."

She gave me Elton John's business number in L.A. and asked me to notify Ryan's pal Michael Jackson and would I also "please call Judy."

"Judy who?" I asked.

"Judith Light."

I quickly jotted down all the phone numbers, said that I believed Ryan was right, there was a "chance," and swallowed hard as my own voice began to quiver.

Judith Light played the role of Jeanne in *The Ryan White Story* on ABC-TV. Both Ryan and his mom were on the set during the shooting; Ryan even had a small scene with Lukas Haas, who played him. Ryan loved being part of the movie business, and everybody on the set was crazy about the kid whose real teenage life they were re-creating. Judy was especially taken with the two flesh-and-blood characters in this mother-son drama, so when she answered the phone, I tried to be gentle and stammered a little as I shaped the bulletin. The word "respirator" put an arrow in her heart.

"I'll call her right now," Judy said.

In a corner room of the Pediatric Intensive Care Unit, Ryan's underdeveloped body had turned pale and begun to bloat. The only sound was the rhythmic *woosh* of the motor that forced air into the body cavity through a hose taped to his mouth. Needles pierced his unconscious body everywhere, including the big toe on his left foot. Doctors and nurses wearing Styrofoam masks and plastic face shields gave this room of mercy the hard industrial look of a foundry.

As she watched from a distance that would not impede the team of would-be lifesavers, Jeanne White took another bullet, one of many that had been fired from all directions in the five-year odyssey that began at Christmastime in 1984, when she was told that her son had AIDS.

"As long as there's a chance, Mom," Ryan had said.

Now, as she watched mechanically forced air create blood-colored mucus bubbles at the nostrils of her only son, a crushing heaviness deepened an already unbearable depression. Were those the last words Ryan would ever speak? Would she carry for the rest of her life another ache in her heart? She never said good-bye.

At the cemetery, I joined five other pallbearers, including Los Angeles Raider Howie Long, in effortlessly lifting the wasted remains of another victim of the most devastating global health emergency of my time.

What follows is the story of a single mother, a middle-class resident of America's heartland, a Bible-believing Methodist and member of the United Auto Workers Union, who wanted nothing more than to raise her children well and pay her bills. In the early eighties, as she sent her children off to school and punched the time clock at the Delco plant in Kokomo, she could not have known that a contaminated blood product would infect her hemophiliac son with the AIDS virus and propel her into a world of the strange alphabet of AIDS and AZT and T cells, of lawyers and school boards, and of homophobia. Ryan found the word "fag" scribbled on his school locker, while anonymous callers shouted obscenities at Jeanne on a local radio station. Here is a woman who was desperately trying to keep her son alive, coping with a bullet hole in her living room window and all the while keeping the flame of motherhood burning equally under *both* her children even as Big Media rushed blindly past her daughter Andrea in search of still more feature stories on "The Boy with AIDS."

Although Jeanne White's story took her from Midwestern obscurity to photo ops with Elizabeth Taylor and other American glitterati, she never missed Andrea's roller-skating competitions, even when *Newsweek* was camped in her front yard.

This is a woman who learned who her friends were, the hard way.

What follows on these pages is more than the story of a single-parent family struggling with AIDS. It is a celebration of the unflagging spirit of a woman who has survived life's biggest sucker punch and who remains determined to be a good mother to Andrea, to nourish her happy new marriage and to insure that her son is remembered not for how he died, but for how he lived.

Today, when Jeanne speaks the truth about the virus to students of all levels from coast to coast, she has come to save their lives. And when the crowds gather in gymnasiums, it pleases her to know that the young people in the audience have come, not to see Jeanne, but to see "Ryan's mom."

"Dear Lord, please let me do Ryan proud..."

My son, Ryan, was buried on April 11, 1990. The trees had already begun to bud. But there was no spring in Indiana that day. The clouds hung gray and heavy. A sudden hailstorm chilled everyone, pounding like bullets on the big black cars and the pavement. All the papers carried pictures of the large crowd of fifteen hundred people who actually managed to come inside the Second Presbyterian Church in Indianapolis, and the hundreds more who kept a vigil outside, and the pallbearers—including Phil Donahue; Elton John; Howie Long of the Los Angeles Raiders; my brother, Thomas Hale, and brother-in-law, Leo Joseph; and Ryan's best friend, John

Huffman—who carried Ryan's coffin. I still remember that some stray ray of sunshine glittered on Elton's black sequined cap.

I was in shock. I couldn't accept that my little boy was gone. The truth is that, through everything, I had never really believed that Ryan would die. From the moment just before Christmas 1984, when I was told that he had contracted AIDS from the Factor needed to control his hemophilia, to the moment he died at the age of eighteen, I had always felt sure he would be healed, that he would survive long enough for a cure to be found. Not wanting to appear faithless, I had never planned his funeral. That was why I was so helpless when the time came, so utterly dependent on others to make the arrangements.

In that open coffin, Ryan looked so thin and young. It was as though the illness had taken him back from being an eighteen-year-old and made him seem like a small child again. We dressed him the way he would have wanted—pop-star style—with his sharp, reflective sunglasses, in his favorite red shirt and his faded jean jacket.

The Second Presbyterian Church in Indianapolis had been selected—actually by Elton John—because it was so spacious, with room enough for Ryan's many friends from Hamilton Heights High School in Arcadia, which had canceled classes so the children could attend. It was a big, beautiful building of pale brown stone, with a rose window in the front and a broad lawn all around and perfectly trimmed evergreens hugging the walls. In the large room off to the back, the celebrities and the media who had flocked to Ryan's cause could gather away from the general public. Tons of famous, important people seated themselves in the sanctuary. Truthfully, I'm not sure that I was sufficiently gracious to them, because I felt so dazed, exhausted and unable to concentrate.

I kept thinking how different this church was from the smaller

Methodist church in Kokomo which our family had attended for three generations and where Ryan might more rightfully have been buried. We had left Kokomo in 1987, on the heels of a bitter confrontation with some citizens there who did not want Ryan to attend school with their kids because he had AIDS. We had fought for Ryan's right to go to school, and in the end, we had won. But on the way to our bleak victory we had made a lot of enemies—and some of them attended our church. So when he was sick, stinging from the pain of rejection, Ryan had made me promise that at his funeral, the Reverend Bud Probasco, then senior pastor at the Center Chapel United Methodist Church in Pendleton, Indiana, would lead the service instead of our regular minister. Strange—for a boy *not* to be buried in his family's church in his hometown with his own preacher. Funny, how things turn out.

My daughter, Andrea—then sixteen years old—reined in her tears with an iron self-control that she had learned from close acquaintance with discrimination and suffering. Beautiful, blond, strong and athletic, a roller-skating champion since her childhood, she had been better able to withstand public rejection than some others in our family. My mother, Gloria Hale, had nearly collapsed from it. My father, Tom, a salt-of-the-earth heartlander, had never quite recovered from the moment in church when an old friend had refused to hold Ryan's hand during an Easter prayer. My sister, Janet, and her husband, Leo Joseph, had come up from Birmingham with their three daughters; my brother, Tom, and his wife, Debbie, stood nearby with their four children. The family members formed a wall of strength around me and Andrea, as they always had.

Michael Jackson, who had been a buddy and a comfort to Ryan, came and stood beside me. When it got really hard for me, he was there for me to lean on. Michael's people and Elton John's people had worried that some fans might come, not to pay their last respects to Ryan, but to see the celebrities; that these people might yell and scream as though they were at a rock concert instead of a funeral. We were all real pleased that nobody did that; that everybody gave Ryan respect.

On the cover of the funeral program were the traditional words from John that accompany a Service of Witness to the Resurrection. "Jesus said: 'I am the resurrection and the life; he who believes in me, though he die, yet shall he live, and whoever lives and believes in me shall never die.'" Also on the cover was Ryan's picture, and under it the words that had so greatly comforted all of us who mourned for him: "I know I'm goin' to a Better Place."

The President's wife, Mrs. Barbara Bush, came to the funeral, representing a government which at long last had decided to make a public recognition that AIDS was ravaging the nation and the world. Many of the folks we had come to know through the television movie about Ryan's struggle came as well, among them Lukas Haas, who played Ryan; Judith Light, who played me; Linda Otto, the producer.

Governor Evan Bayh, who had called Ryan "an American hero," had ordered all the flags in Indiana to fly at half-mast. Helicopters buzzed overhead. The whole ceremony was carried live on television. Dr. Woodrow A. Myers Jr., who had been Health Commissioner of Indiana when Ryan took sick, was interviewed on the news. "Instead of living his short life in peace and harmony with those around him," he told a reporter, "Ryan, his mother, Jeanne, and his sister, Andrea, were forced to confront the angry venom of fear from neighbors, strangers and from public officials who preferred to remain comfortable, cloaked in their mutual ignorance." Dr. Myers had always seen our family's struggle in the context of a greater American struggle for freedom from fear.

I was astonished to see David Rosselot at the church. He had served as attorney for the Concerned Citizens group that was ready to do just about anything to keep Ryan out of school until he died. His wife, Marsha, stood right next to him. My recollection of Marsha was captured in the pictures of her that had appeared in the newspaper, in which she was marching proudly to the bank with nineteen thousand dollars in a paper bag that the parents' group had raised to fight Ryan's return to school, or celebrating, when the judge granted the restraining order that kept Ryan home, with her arms held high in a gesture of joyous victory.

It really meant a lot to me that they had come today. David Rosselot gave me a hug and said, "Mrs. White, this is one case I wish I had never taken."

On the long line outside, folks stood patiently in the rain, waiting to get in. One of them was a neighbor of ours, Roy Ginder, who had come with his children. Roy was a mechanic and an autobody expert who had helped Ryan class up the beautiful red Ford Mustang that Michael Jackson had given him, which he never really got to drive much but loved more than anything he possessed in this world. It was sitting on the front lawn of our home in the lakeside community of Cicero, among wreaths of flowers, a fitting memorial to a car-crazy kid. When Ryan was stuck at home, too sick to attend school, he would drag himself down to the Ginders' house and gab about motors and treads while Roy worked on some old wreck in his driveway. They even talked about Ryan someday going to work as an apprentice in the body shop where Roy worked—if only someday would ever come.

The Ginder family never made it into the church. Just as they approached the doors, it was announced that the last seat had been filled.

Some of the people who couldn't get in gathered under the wide gray sky and sang "Amazing Grace" for my boy. Inside, Robert Shapfer led the Sanctuary Choir, and the Hamilton Heights High choir sang "That's What Friends Are For." Those twelve sweet girls had only two days to rehearse that song. They wept as they sang their hearts out. To me, their voices were just beautiful.

A Kokomo woman who had been a great, often anonymous friend to our family and our cause—Marcia Blacklidge—gave her seat in the church to a devastated stranger. It was a quiet generosity characteristic of Marcia.

Elton John sent a wreath of roses, dozens and dozens of red roses in the shape of a heart, with a border of baby's breath. I swear I've never seen anything like it. Across the roses was a message in red ribbons: "Dear Ryan. You will always be with me. You have touched so many people. Thank you. I love you. Elton." The wreath stood near Ryan's open coffin at the funeral home. When we set all the flowers out at the gravesite, we took some of the roses and wrote Ryan's name in them. I still have one of those roses; I'll keep it always.

Carrie Jackson Van Dyke, who had come to know Ryan when she was a TV reporter and had become a close friend and a spokesperson for our family, recalls that the sun came out suddenly, just as the minister began to pray over Ryan's coffin.

All along the thirty-five-mile funeral route to Cicero, on Highway 31, people were standing, stopped in their vehicles, gathered in crowds at every intersection. Folks stood in front of the fast-food places with their hands over their hearts; leaned out of the windows of office buildings and waved good-bye to Ryan. Phil Donahue tells the story that he was riding in the funeral procession and chanced to look out the car window. He saw one of the state troopers who had been assigned to traffic control standing in the middle of the intersection, saluting. The sight put a lump in Phil's throat; tears rolled down his face. They still do when he thinks of that lone mourner saluting on the country road. It was Phil who would become my most treasured guide and adviser in setting up the Ryan White Foundation for AIDS Education and shaping Ryan's legacy.

Reverend Probasco told how we had not received the miracle cure we had hoped for, but that "God gave us a miracle in Ryan. He healed the wounded spirit and made it whole."

"Many of you here are very successful," he continued. "Your lives are filled with glamour and fame. Yet you brought Ryan and his cause into your lives and aided him in his mission and showed us how to do the same.

"Now I challenge all of us to accept his faith. For, you see, Ryan was successful, too, in getting all of us involved. He helped us to care and to believe that with God's help, nothing is impossible— even for a kid." The minister quoted Ryan himself, urging everyone to "make AIDS a disease—not a dirty word."

Elton sat at a grand piano up at the front of the church. There was a picture of Ryan on the piano, the one of him with the spiky haircut and the big smile that I loved best. Elton sang a hymn and played a song of his called "Skyline Pigeon." The song brought me an image of Ryan's spirit "turned loose" from his fate, flying "off to distant lands."

I remember every single thing about that funeral: the sincerity, the inspiring words, the grief, the beautiful singing. And yet, in a strange way, I felt that I wasn't even present. I felt like I was floating above the funeral, a witness to some bizarre dream. There in that big stone church, it seemed impossible that all this commotion was about my smart, funny kid with the blond cowlick. I saw him thundering along on his tricycle down the street from Grandma's house. I saw him lining up his matchbox cars for a big race on the kitchen floor. I saw him healthy. Before AIDS.

You think you're prepared. You think you've rehearsed the loss in your mind so much that you must surely know it cold by now. But you cannot know it until it happens. A blank emptiness comes into your life, sort of like a fog. You lose focus. I felt that Ryan's absence was temporary, as though he was at school or out with his friends and would soon be coming back; that he was just away, but not gone. I wandered around the house looking for my child, looking for his eighteen years. If somebody spoke to me, I could hardly hear; that was how loud the grieving roared in my head.

I lived in terror of forgetting. Believe me, it wasn't a silly fear. Forgetting really happens. Your mind rebels against the grief and shuts down and for minutes at a time, you cannot see your dear one's face. That's why we keep so many pictures, those of us who have lost children. Not to worship the dead or anything neurotic like that, but just to jump-start our memories, to be always reminded.

The worst thing about losing a young person is that the loss keeps on happening. It happened when Ryan died . . . and it happened again when Christmas came and his stocking didn't have to be stuffed. It happened again when his friends started getting married and having babies, and I realized that I would never own that particular joy.

Loneliness was not my problem, at least not at first. I had company for weeks after the funeral: Andrea, Mom and Dad, my brother and sister. Our friend Greg Louganis, the great Olympic diving champion, hadn't been able to make it to the service, so he came later and stayed a few days. Matt Frewer, the hilarious actor who had played Coke's Max Headroom, had befriended Ryan and quietly, without any fanfare, had supported and encouraged us for years, came by a week later. My friends Mary Baker and Betsy Stewart stopped in every other minute, wanting to know what they could do to help. John Huffman, Ryan's buddy, had also become a close friend of Andrea's; he stayed with us for several weeks, distracting her with talk and fun. Oh, yes, we had quite a lot of comforters around us. It was sad, but it was bonding, with hours of reminiscing, hours of tears.

At the same time there was this big emptiness in my chest. I kept thinking: *Why did he die? Why wasn't there a miracle? Why did he get sick in the first place? Why was he chosen to suffer so much? Why are all the people who made him so miserable—the school officials and teachers and bigoted parents, the hate radio hosts, the people who shot at our house and sent us pornographic letters—still out there, enjoying pleasant, uneventful lives?* It made no sense to me. I couldn't piece it all together.

I had a lot of trouble with Andrea when Ryan died. She and her brother had been very close. In a hostile world, they kept each other going. Even if he was just sick on the couch, lying around waiting for her to arrive from school and report on the goings-on in the normal, regular teenage world, even such a little presence had given shape to her day. He had been sick so often, and he had always gotten better, and I guess she believed he always would.

Now he was gone for good. Now just coming home was painful for her, because he wasn't there. For over a week, she would stay out late and not come through the door until it was time to go to bed. I felt that I was losing my daughter! Like most mothers of sick children, I had always lived in terror that something would happen to my well child too. I was probably over protective of Andrea as a result. I was afraid that she was going to get involved with the wrong people, that she might start drinking or trying drugs because she was so depressed. I was afraid she was rebelling because she had lost Ryan and now she didn't care what happened to herself—as though she wanted to punish herself for being the well child, the one who was still alive.

Finally one night—it was past eleven o'clock—I stopped her when she came in and said, "Andrea! We have to talk!" And I sat her down and made her talk to me.

She said: "AIDS took my brother's life. We lived with AIDS every day for five and a half years. I don't care if I ever hear the word 'AIDS' again."

I realized that she wasn't getting in with a bad crowd. She was just running. Trying to distract herself. Trying to adjust her vision and see her future in a different light. She stayed out with John and her other friends until late in the night, in an effort to manage her grief and make a new sense of how to grow up and who to be.

When the welcome guests left and went home to their own houses, and Andrea went out with her friends, I sat in Ryan's room and looked at old pictures, played old videotapes, read and reread the wonderful letters I had received.

It seemed to me that I could read the history of our times in those letters, that all the characters in my life had passed through the prism of that funeral. I had a letter from Donald Almquist, the CEO of Delco Electronics, where I had worked for almost twenty-five years; where I had met my first husband, Wayne White, and my second husband, Steve Ford; where I had ended my factory days in a storm of slander and ridicule. "Ryan seemed almost invincible,"

Mr. Almquist wrote. ". . . he will always represent courage in the face of ignorance."

I had seen a country that had never heard of AIDS, that had treated it with ignorance and superstition, learn and grow and accept and, to some extent, deal. A letter from President George Bush said that my Ryan had had a part in that. "With his good nature, and clear-sightedness," the President wrote, Ryan had "helped to educate our nation."

One letter from Hal Wingo, the assistant managing editor of *People* magazine, which had always given Ryan so much support, just haunted me.

"I don't doubt that God knew what He was doing by making you Ryan's mother," Hal wrote. "You can—and should—live the rest of your life in the absolute certainty that you were chosen for this purpose and that you gave him the most important things he needed to face his situation with all the strength and dignity he always demonstrated."

If that was true—if God had put me here to be Ryan's mom—then what was I to do with my life now that Ryan was gone?

Reverend Probasco had said that death was like when you play hard all day and come inside and fall asleep on your parents' bed and eventually you wake up and find that you're all tucked in your own bed because your father has lifted you in his strong arms while you were sleeping and carried you there. Ryan, he said, had fallen asleep and God had lifted him up in His big, strong arms and carried him to his Heavenly rest.

I knew he was in a better place. I knew it with all my heart. What I could not find was *my* place. How would I know my task? How would I recognize my direction now?

During Ryan's last hospital stay, Dr. Martin Kleiman of James Whitcob Riley Hospital for Children called to say that Senator Ted Kennedy of Massachusetts was trying to get hold of me.

Dr. Kleiman is a slender, retiring man with a neat gray beard. He does not get real excited about things, but on this occasion he did go so far as to say: "I think it's something you might be interested in. They're trying to pass a bill in the Senate to help AIDS victims, and they want to name it after Ryan."

I told Senator Kennedy's office that it was fine with me. AIDS had been public knowledge since the early eighties. By the time Ryan passed away, 81,000 people had died from it and a million more were HIV-positive in our country alone. Yet no legislation had ever been passed appropriating funds for the special needs—including the high-priced drugs—of people with AIDS. This new bill would provide home health care for AIDS sufferers. It would help them with such things as transportation to the clinics where their drugs were dispensed, and pay for the drugs, too. It would provide them with visiting nurses and homemakers, and would underwrite the cost of portable IV equipment and hospital beds and other gadgetry which would keep the AIDS patients out of the hospital as long as humanly possible, making their lives more comfortable and allowing them to stay close to those who loved them until the last possible minute. Because there was so much news coverage about Ryan during the weeks surrounding his death, the bill finally received the media attention it deserved, and that improved its chances for passage.

But there is more to passing a bill than just a mention on the evening news. Senator Kennedy wanted me to come personally to Washington, to help him and others lobby for its passage.

I said: "No, I can't do it. I'm not smart enough. I would just mess up everything." It was only a few days after Ryan's funeral. I had no courage left. I was drained. Thousands of letters were piling up in my house that I didn't even have the strength to open and read. I felt sad, empty, angry. I wanted to scream. If I went to Washington, I might just break down emotionally and create a scene. I felt like I wasn't in control of myself.

But the lobbyists persisted, which is what they're good at and why they're lobbyists. Senator Kennedy's staff called me. Terry Beirn, whom I just adored, pleaded with me to make the trip. Terry had been my first close gay friend. He and the other folks at AmFAR (the American Foundation for AIDS Research) had stood by me and Ryan and Andrea when nobody else would look our way; they had become close friends and colleagues. It was hard to turn Terry down—but I was so fearful of screwing up, walking into some important Senator's office and opening my mouth to speak and bursting into tears. I was afraid that because of my inexperience, I would hurt the very cause I wanted to help, so once again I said no.

Then Senator Kennedy called me himself.

He told me that I needn't be afraid, that I was just a mom talking to people who happened to be U.S. Senators about what it was like to lose a child to AIDS. He said: "We have twenty-three Senators we'd like you to approach, Mrs. White." That about scared me to death. I continued to say no.

Senator Orrin Hatch of Utah, the cosponsor of the Ryan White CARE Act, called me the next day and tried to reassure me some more. They would brief me, he said. They'd tell me everything I needed to know. Politics was just people, plain people after all.

Senator Hatch's confident words lingered in my mind.

"You're a strong woman, Mrs. White. I know you can do it."

Ryan's words echoed in my memory.

"I'm not afraid of dying," he had said once on one of Phil Donahue's programs. ". . . it's how you live your life that counts."

If he hadn't been afraid of dying, then how could I be afraid of twenty-three Senators?

So finally I called everybody back and said, "Okay."

I went to Washington and, one by one, I met with the Senators. I said to them: "I am here to ask you to support my boy's bill. I don't know anything about politics, about filibusters or lobbying, or how any of this happens. But I know what it is to lose a child . . . and there are other people out there just like me, losing their children, losing everything . . . and we have to help them." I got so tired after a while, I could hardly stand. Tom Sheridan, the Public Policy Director of the AIDS Action Council, brought me a sandwich and sat me down in the Senate anteroom and kept pointing out Senators whom I should approach. I talked to each one individually. One by one, they concluded that they had to vote for the bill.

Terry Beirn and Tom Sheridan and Mike Itzkowitz from Senator Kennedy's office really wanted me to speak with Senator Jesse Helms of North Carolina, whose opposition to helping people with AIDS was well known. Finally I ran into him on an elevator.

"My name is Jeanne White, I'm Ryan White's mother. I'd really like to be able to talk to you."

He scowled at me like a grumpy old bear.

"Call my office. Call my office."

When we called his office, we were told that he would not meet with me. I felt bad, but I learned that his rejection wouldn't destroy my confidence. I learned that I could talk to important strangers. I learned that I could speak up at a press conference. I felt like I did okay, that I sure could have done better, but it wasn't real bad. Talking to the Senators made me feel very hopeful. I will never forget the meeting I had with Senator Joe Biden from Delaware. He talked about losing members of his family in a horrendous car accident. He understood what it was for thousands and thousands of American parents to be losing their children to the nightmare of AIDS while an unresponsive government stood silently by.

Finally, we collected sixty-one cosponsors for the bill. But the Senate leadership was still not bringing it to the floor for a vote. I sat up in the Senate gallery all day long, just praying and waiting and watching to see what would happen. At last the bill got to the floor and was passed by huge margins in both the House and the Senate.

I believe now that that trip to Washington (it turned out to be one of several I would make) to help the lobbying effort on the Ryan White CARE Act (CARE stands for Comprehensive AIDS Resource Emergency) was the most transforming thing I ever did. It made me feel for the first time that I could do something in my own right, that I could be part of important events the way my son had been. I felt such a sense of accomplishment and personal reward, such enormous satisfaction, because I was finally able to give back something to all the people who had stood by us and helped us in our struggle.

As I walked down the long, stony corridors of the Senate Office Building, my steps growing more determined, my voice growing stronger, I couldn't help wondering how in the world I had arrived at this point. How had it happened that my boy Ryan had so inspired his country that I was now obligated to carry on in his name? All I had wanted to do was sit around in a room and grieve and feel sorry for myself. But now I didn't totally possess my own life (maybe no parent ever does). I couldn't just hoard the memory of my son. He had given me a new work. He had made me, by his suffering and courage, a new woman.

All through that time in Washington, I kept saying to myself: *Dear Lord, please help me do Ryan proud.*

Looking back at where I had started—a shy, chunky kid in Kokomo, playing house with her mom, expecting nothing but an ordinary little life—I couldn't believe how much I had learned, how far I had come.

Chapter 1

We All Get Tested in This Life

I sure wonder sometimes how a person manages in this tricky, hard world without a family. Life has taught me that if you lose your family, you've lost everything. And if you have a family to love you and support you and stand by you, it almost doesn't make any difference how much you lose, you're always a winner in the end.

My mother, Gloria Hale, was born and raised in Kokomo, Indiana. Her grandparents had been farmers in Germany. They settled first in Louisville, Kentucky, and then moved out to Indiana. Mom's father died young, when she was only nine. That left Grandma

Helen with nine children, six girls and three boys, to raise pretty much on her own.

They had a house and a yard, but beyond that, not much more than the bare necessities of life. Mom always says they had oatmeal for breakfast, lunch and dinner, and they each received one pair of shoes a year. They'd go out in the yard and eat the vegetables right out of the garden. The church would help out sometimes by donating used clothing to the family. It's the same exact Methodist church that we went to—St. Luke's. Mom remembers Grandma Helen tearing apart the old coats and making them over so they'd fit her kids. The big ones took care of the little ones. The little ones did whatever chores they could. Those old enough to work brought every dollar they could back to the family.

Evenings they'd all sit around and Grandma Helen would sing to her children or iron or sew while they talked about all the wonderful dresses and bikes they would buy when Grandma Helen's chain letter came in. Of course, Grandma Helen's chain letter, with the thousands of dollars she hoped for, never came in. But just having something to hope for and dream about was all the fun in the world for her children.

No matter that they were so poor, Grandma Helen never turned away from a beggar's outstretched hand. During the Depression, when there were so many down-and-out people on the road looking for work, she would invite any stranger into her house for toast and coffee. She was never afraid. She told my mom: "When a stranger comes to the door, even if it's someone who seems not right in the head, you should help that person, because you never know if he or she might not be a messenger of the Lord, or even the Lord Himself."

As a child, I felt a little disappointed that Grandma Helen didn't live very close by. I wanted a grandma like the kids across the street had, who came over with presents on holidays, whose visits were always bountiful, special occasions.

But as I matured and started out to set up my own household, I realized that what Grandma Helen had given us was a lot more important than presents. She had given us an ideal of family—a vision of the way people ought to treat each other, on which we could model our own families and design the standards and manners inside our own homes. Her kids had nothing, but they never felt poor. Because the family was their riches, and their mother's love was what they could take to the bank.

The story in our family is that Dad fell in love with Mom just from looking at her. Mom was working at a restaurant called The White Hut. My dad—Thomas Edward Hale—was working at Kroger's Market, a big chain of supermarkets out our way. He had quit school at sixteen to go to work because his dad died and he had no choice. He went and had lunch at The White Hut one day when they were serving peanut butter cream pie. All the customers were raising hell because the pie was spoiled and sour. Mom came over and asked Dad if he had any problem with the pie. He had no idea what she was talking about. He had been staring at her so intently that he had just gobbled up the awful pie without even tasting it.

My folks married when they were scarcely twenty years old, and started out life together in a ramshackle apartment on Jasper Street. The war would have lifted some years out of Dad's life, but he was so deaf (from what cause he has no idea) that the Army wouldn't take him. First I was born, then my sister, Janet, then my brother, Tommy Joe. Mom stayed home and took care of us, except when she worked canning tomatoes at the Libby's factory. It was seasonal work: ten weeks; just long enough for her to earn the money to buy our school clothes.

Dad rose up through the ranks at Kroger's and stayed there for forty-three years, straight up until he retired. He once figured out that no less than seven members of our family had worked at Kroger's. A loyal union man, and an Eisenhower Democrat, he was the union steward at the store and soon became the produce manager. He was famous for his displays at the store. With Mom's help—she eventually worked there as head cashier—he would make these incredible arrangements of fruits and vegetables. Millions of mushrooms! Towers of oranges! Popcorn cascading over pyramids of soda cans! Dad's displays were so enticing and beautiful, they would win prizes from the Kroger's chain. They kept offering to make him manager, but he always turned down the job, preferring a little less money and responsibility and more time and freedom to do some of the things he loved.

I idolized my mother. It seemed to me she did everything that a good mom should—she made great chicken-and-noodles, she did lovely handiwork, she gave out excellent advice and she always had a dollar or two of her own in her pocket that she had earned. She was a Brownie Scout leader and then a Girl Scout leader; she got me involved in the camps and the crafts, and I had qualified for all the badges. I can remember all through high school being very proud of Mom, because she looked so young and pretty, and she was so active in the community. If somebody asked her to help out—even if it was with the dirty work, the cleanup in the kitchen—she would do it willingly, without ever seeking attention or recognition.

I was aware that money was tight. However it seemed to me we never lacked for anything we wanted, and honestly, by today's standards, we didn't want a lot. We might have to save up for it, or wait for it, but eventually we got it. We all had a clear sense of how hard our parents worked and how they shared everything with us. So we shared back.

Whenever I went to the store to buy candy, even when I was real little, maybe six or seven years old, I'd always keep a nickel or a dime to buy some tiny little knickknack for my mom as well. I can remember the smile of delight on her face when I came running home with those gifts for her. She acted as though they were the most precious things in the world.

Every supper meal we had meat, potatoes, vegetable and a dessert. The rule was that you couldn't eat dessert until after supper. Mom made an exception for me because I liked chocolate pudding on my fried potatoes. So she'd give me a scoop ahead of time, and I would gobble it up while my brother and sister made "yuchhh!" faces and my father covered his eyes. We always could have more if we wanted, before Mom and Dad did. On the other hand, if there was something we knew Dad liked and we saw there wasn't enough, we automatically left him the seconds, without anybody discussing it or even thinking twice about it.

Mom fixed the meal. When she was working, we kids would always do the dishes. We'd argue like everybody does about whose turn it was and who would wash and who would dry. Eventually a fair arrangement emerged.

We always said a little prayer before dinner. It was truly meaningful. My parents really were grateful to God for being able to take good care of their children.

When I look back on the family system now, it seems like a collection of small things—sharing the work, sharing the money, making allowances for this preference and that nutty peculiarity, not taking blessings for granted, being grateful, giving gifts with joy. But it's those small habits from home that prepare you for the world.

My very favorite game as a little girl was playing house with my mother. She'd be ironing and I would pretend I was the neighbor "Mrs. Jones" who had come to pay her a visit. I'd sit right there by the ironing board and we'd talk about our tea parties and our children and all the things that neighbors used to talk about in what now appears to be a totally bygone day.

I couldn't wait to grow up and become "Mrs. Jones," for that beautiful, comfortable fantasy of motherhood and homemaking to be my real life. I longed to have a big dollhouse, with lots of rooms and little miniature people, that I could decorate and arrange into my own vision of homey paradise.

Mom is a spiritual person, a tower of empathy, a believer in the magic of love and the love of God. She tells the story that when I was born, they had to perform a cesarean section and gave her too much anesthetic, and for a while, she actually died. She saw the light and the tunnel that everybody talks about, but she never entered the tunnel. She felt she was floating over the room in this cloud. She looked down and saw Grandma Helen and Dad and they were crying. Then all of a sudden they were gone . . . and she regained consciousness.

Years later, when I gave birth to Ryan and began hemorrhaging uncontrollably, she prayed for me. And when the bleeding got so bad that I was about to exit this world, a wonderful sense of happiness and peace came over her. "I would not have felt that peace," she says, "if anything bad was going to happen to my Jeanne." And to this day, she believes that her "Sense of Peace" was really a vision of my recovery.

Mom always loved dolls and figurines. When Ryan took sick, that was when she started her collection of Precious Moments figurines. They are statues of little children, paled to angel whiteness, and each carries a message of tenderness and faith.

I caught the collecting bug from Mom. True to my dollhouse dreams, I now spend hours and hours assembling miniature villages that I populate with tiny porcelain people and illuminate with twinkling lights. The shelves and bookcases in my house are bursting with pictures and mementos.

Every time my children bought me something or wrote me a letter, I kept it, treasured it, displayed it, for it represented a time in our lives that wanted to be remembered. I never threw away my kids' old toys—Andrea's dolls, Ryan's books. I nest them in garlands of holly at Christmas. I make chains of the blocks and beads they played with, and hang them on the mantel. I write the names of everyone in my family on a Santa's list made of accounting tape and string them through the branches of the Christmas tree. My home at Christmas says everything about me. What is the holiday about anyway except family and memories?

Maybe you would see my collections and say: "This woman is living in a dream of days gone by."

But I tell you, when the world is too cruel, your happy memories are the best place to go for solace.

We moved to the house on Fisher Street when I was around seven years old. It was our first house, a small flat model in what we call "an addition," a development in the suburbs of Kokomo. I remember just loving it, and thinking we must be real rich now that we were moving there. The house cost $8,600. The down payment was $600.

Everybody was the same as us in our addition. Same-age kids, same financial situation. Same race, same religion, same politics.

There were no Communists around, no KKK members, no criminals or homosexuals. Dad and Mom even swear that there were no adulterers, but I believe that about as much as I believe the rest. Whoever was "different" in any way must have been in deep hiding. That was just the way things were in the suburbs of Kokomo, Indiana, in the fifties. If there was anything to gossip about, my parents never did it in front of us.

After a few years, my dad got together with some of his friends and built a garage. I don't think he had any special training in building, but I do think the Hales generally had clever, gifted hands. We all could have gone into creative professions—because we had a family knack for it—if only we had listened to our parents and acquired the right training.

For me, Mom planned a career as an interior decorator because she felt I really had some talent. She begged me to go to art school. However, at eighteen, I was determined to stop studying and go to work and get married and have the happy-homemaker life I had played at as a little girl.

So I ignored my mother's advice and I never went to art school, to my eternal regret.

Dad loved the outdoors. He was cofounder of the Kokomo Bass Anglers Club and wrote articles for their magazine. As long as I can remember, we'd take picnics and go on fishing expeditions and spend the whole day in some guy's pond or woods. For a couple of years, we had a tiny trailer up at Bruce Lake. Janet and I slept on a bed that converted to a kitchen table. Tommy Joe often slept outside in a tent with his friends. Mom fried the fish that Dad caught for dinner. No meal tasted as good as a plate full of Mom's fried bluegill or bass.

Sometimes Dad went on fishing trips with buddies. A lot of

times he would go out by himself, leave in the evening and stay out on the lake all night long. Mom would be just petrified—because he couldn't swim. *What if a storm comes up? What if the boat hits some rock and springs a leak?* She'd be up until dawn, fretting. Me, I was just fascinated.

"What happens to you out there, Dad? Why do you love it so?"

"It's the feel of the sun and the wind," he said. "It's the quiet. It's watching the night sky so full of shooting stars, makes you just know there's got to be a better Being someplace behind all this."

When I was in fourth grade, Mom began to think there might be something wrong with me. My skin looked dry to her. It was crisscrossed with lines, "kind of like a dried-up lake" she told the doctor. I was puffy. I wasn't eating much, but I was gaining weight. The doctor said nothing was wrong. It got worse in the fifth grade, and the sixth, and the seventh. All the kids were going to The Seashore, which was a big swimming pool in our town. I just didn't want to go. I didn't have the energy, and besides, I didn't like the way I looked in a bathing suit.

I was getting to be a big, heavy girl in a family of slender people, and it was happening to me just at the time when I was entering my early teens, becoming interested in boys and how I looked. I used to have nightmares that I would end up like my seventh-grade teacher, Miss Flora. She was real, real heavy. Everybody made fun of her. The backs of her legs hung clear to the floor. It sounds impossible. But everybody who studied in her class remembers that.

Finally Mom got me to Dr. Craig. He took one look at me and said, "This girl's got thyroid problems."

They put me in the hospital for two weeks and did all these tests and finally figured out how they could regulate my thyroid. I had never been in the hospital before, never had a broken limb or stitches or anything. Yes, I was scared—and I didn't like the needles and the blood work all the time—but I wasn't deathly sick and so the experience had the effect of dispelling my natural fear of hospitals and making me trust medical people. They made me better. The puffiness and the dryness went away. My weight became my personal problem, not some mysterious disorder. My energy returned.

On the other hand, I had this voice of doubt in the family that kept me from thinking that doctors were invincible. It belonged to my father's sister, my feisty, independent-minded Aunt Thelma, whom I just adored. I used to baby-sit for her sons when I was about thirteen, just when the thyroid thing was happening to me. Aunt Thelma's little boy wasn't feeling so good, so she took him to a hospital and the doctors decided he had leukemia. Another mother would have collapsed at such news. Not Aunt Thelma. She said, "These doctors don't know what they're talking about. My boy does not have leukemia." And she was right. He didn't.

I think we have to listen to our physicians. Most of the time, they know what they are talking about. But there are times when your body— or even your heart—tells you that they are wrong. And I always told my children: "You have to listen to your body. You have to listen to your heart."

As a teenager, I was almost hysterically shy. In my fantasies I looked like my idol, Annette Funicello. My dream was to get my hair to flip up just like Marlo Thomas's in *That Girl*. But in true, everyday life, public appearances terrified me. When I represented

Kmart in the Miss Howard County Contest, I agonized over having to model clothes in front of all the shoppers.

My shape conditioned my self-image. I felt bad about myself because I was squat and chunky, and I did everything I could to make people like me in spite of that. I was famous for being a pushover. When I baby-sat for folks, I'd clean their house, too. It got to be that many people would leave their house real dirty because they knew I was coming.

I did manage to become involved in swimming and actually participated in water ballet. But my big fun activity was Yell Block, a five-hundred-person cheering section at Kokomo High School home basketball games. We wore blue skirts, red tops and white gloves, and did synchronized hand movements that spelled out messages for the folks in the stands on the opposite side of the field. In sports-crazy Indiana, Yell Block was the closest thing to a team for me.

I was always jealous of my willowy younger sister, Janet, who appeared to be able to eat anything and never gain an ounce. I wanted to be a cheerleader, but I just couldn't do it. Janet, a natural athlete, made the team with ease.

Janet and I shared a room. She was messy. I was neat. We fought constantly. Finally we literally drew a line down the middle of the little room and achieved a truce of separation. When I graduated from high school and went to work, she would wear my clothes. Even though she was so much thinner than I was, she would wait until I left for work and safety-pin great big hunks of my clothes and manage to wear them. She would get out of school before I would get home from work and she'd hang them back in the closet. But a lot of times she'd forget and leave the safety pins in, and I'd find them and figure out what happened and blow my stack.

The interesting thing is that now, when I look back on my

girlhood, it seems like that was just about the outer limits for conflict in our home—me and my sister, yelling at each other over who could wear which sweater. We didn't hate our parents; we didn't hate our brother or each other. We bore no deep and abiding sense of recrimination.

We had, for all intents and purposes, what could be called a happy, loving family.

Although I spurned the idea of art school, I did want to be a teacher. My problem was that I didn't think I was smart enough to go to college. So I put in my application at Delco.

In those days, Delco Electronics Corporation produced automobile engines and audio electronics, including car radios. The plant stretched for miles and employed thousands of people. If you could get on at Delco, you could be assured of a good paycheck and just about the best insurance coverage available to any working person in the United States. My mother, who had always worked at Kroger's before, decided to apply as well. She was hired about the same time as I.

When I was first hired, I worked on the line as a parts stuffer—putting transistors and capacitors into car radios. There were about forty people on the line, all women. First you had to wrap the little three-legged transistors—carefully, since they had real sharp edges. You couldn't wear gloves to protect your hands because then you wouldn't have been able to feel the thing to wrap it right. You also had to make sure the legs weren't touching. Then you stuffed the transistors into the radio. My job was to stuff two transistors and several capacitors.

You would do the same thing over and over and over—six hundred, eight hundred, a thousand sets a day. The bell would ring every twenty seconds and you would have to pass the radio on. You had three spares which didn't have your work done on them yet, so if the lady in front of you got behind, you could always grab a spare and stuff that and you wouldn't have to waste a second waiting for her. The whole line had a quota. The supervisors had it all figured out to where you would always end up with just about the same amount every day.

You adjusted to the pressure and the pace. Some folks got so good they could reach their quota and have time to go off and hide and take a nap. Some people would talk, even read on the line—no one minded as long as you didn't make rejects. There was a loud buzzer for your break, and another loud buzzer that told you that you had to be back in your seat. You'd work clear to the end of the day. Then you'd have one minute to clean up, and the buzzer would ring, and you'd clock out. The buzzer controlled your life.

Sometimes I would wrap coils with black, rubbery stuff. Sometimes I soldered the coils as well—pans and pans and pans full of them each day. Four of us would sit at a table with a pot of hot solder in front of us. You curled the wires, dipped them into the pot, then straightened them out with your hands. You had real thick gloves with leather fingers to wipe off the excess solder. The short wires were easy. But the long wires were harder to handle, and very often the solder would slip and fly and hit someone. There were little screens to separate you from the people across from you. But I still had scars all over my arms from solder burns.

The line is a thing of the past now. Today, machines do the work, and they're all computerized. But only twenty years ago, it was done by hand—and it was rough on the fingers and rougher still on the brain. Your mind really went stale on the line. You did a lot of daydreaming.

The thing I loved about Delco was hearing how different people celebrated their holidays, where they'd go for their vacations, how they handled family issues. I'd always come home with a new recipe, a new crafts idea for the kids in the Sunday school where I taught every week. I'd sit on the line, my hands busily working on electronics while my imagination flew to the little lamb finger puppets I was going to make with the kids on Sunday or the new pop-up book about Jonah I was going to read to them.

I met a lot of single girls at Delco, too, and we sure did have some fun times. Many of my friends were moving into their own apartments, for privacy, they said. But I wasn't much of a partygoer, and I was such a straight arrow, I certainly never dreamed of bringing some guy home with me. So privacy didn't mean much to me, and I preferred to save my money and continue living with my folks.

I think I must have been the most naive, innocent person ever to pass through that factory. Cigarettes smelled bad to me. Beer tasted awful. I never drank liquor. I went to a party with my friends where some people got so smashed they passed out on the floor, and I thought to myself: *Why are they making such fools of themselves? Are they crazy?* I simply did not believe the rumors that I heard on the line. People having group sex, switching spouses at wild parties— *ridiculous!* I thought. I didn't believe that any more than I believed that one of my high school girlfriends was having sex at the golf course every night. Of course, some of these stories turned out to be quite true.

During my first ten years at Delco, mostly women worked on the line. The men had the easier jobs. They were the group leaders, the foremen and the stockroom boys. Sure they worked hard, but they didn't have to live by the buzzer; they could socialize and talk on the job. Then suddenly, about 1975, the whole plant changed.

Women started to be group leaders. Stock watchers. Women started getting the real trade jobs, too—they were even electricians.

I became a parts changer, a job I just loved. When there was something wrong with a radio, the repairman would send it back. The parts changer had to change all the parts which had been labeled as defective or badly installed. So you had to know how to tear down the radio, one part after another, and then reassemble the whole thing from scratch. It was the first time that I had ever had a job which required intelligence and remotely suited my abilities.

It was a funny feeling to be in the middle of that change. I had heard vaguely about women's libbers down in Indianapolis, complaining about this and that. But I certainly didn't consider myself one of them. I was the most nonpolitical person in the world. I never voted, and I don't think I knew who was representing me in Congress. And here my whole life was being transformed by some faraway new political movement.

Like most of the women at Delco, I always thought of my job as temporary, and I looked forward to getting out. I said to myself, *You make good money, and that's fine for now, but when you get married and have children, you'll have enough security to quit.* It never occurred to me that marriage and children would make me so insecure that I wouldn't dare to leave Delco for twenty-three years.

One guy in our community was known to be gay. He had a beautiful singing voice and performed with the choir of his church. I was a very literal woman. I thought the church really meant it when they preached that homosexuality was a sin and gay people were morally out of the loop. I kept wondering why, if this guy was supposed to be such a sinner, he was standing up there at my friend's wedding singing praises to the Lord.

Obviously, some Christians had different ideas from those I had heard all my life—and they were still Christians.

I didn't have short-term boyfriends. If I liked a guy, I usually went with him for a long, long time. I went with my high school boyfriend for three years. When I went to work at Delco, I fell in love with a guy from Georgia who was stationed at Grissom Air Force Base (it was Bunker Hill AFB back then). His name was Wayne Perry. We became engaged. He gave me a beautiful ring. The announcement appeared in the paper. But he got cold feet and broke the engagement.

I was upset and embarrassed in front of all my friends. So when another Wayne—Wayne White—started paying attention to me at work, I was ready to respond.

Wayne White and I had been in the same grade at school. When we were young, he lived a few blocks from me. He was real mischievous and would sometimes get in trouble—not bad trouble, just little, silly stuff. We had a couple of classes together in high school, but I really didn't see him again until he returned from serving in the Army in Germany and became a group leader at Delco.

He asked me if I wanted to go out for a Coke sometime. And we ended up having a regular date. I kind of liked him. He was a good-looking sort of guy, short and skinny, with blue-green eyes and dark hair that he styled real nice. He looked great in jeans. He didn't smoke or drink at the time, which I really liked. He had a neat sense of humor. The only thing that put me off a little was that he cussed a lot, jokingly, for laughs.

We couldn't go out much during the week because I worked days and he worked nights. He'd come in early to see me. I really don't think I was *crazy-crazy* about him, but yes, I did like him, and

I really wanted a new boyfriend. I had been at Delco for three years. I was twenty-one. My friends were getting married. I wasn't so much madly in love as I was ready to move out and be a housewife and have my own things and my own family.

We went together for about three months and then decided to get married.

Wayne and I put off having children for three years, and then as soon as I wanted to, I became pregnant. I was so excited! At that time company policy forced any pregnant worker to take a leave at six months. You didn't have a choice. They gave you six weeks' pay and sent you home to prepare for your baby, and you couldn't come back to work until at least six weeks after the birth. It was nice for a change, being free during the day. I remember walking downtown, buying little things for my child. In those days, doctors couldn't tell the sex of your baby, so I looked for things in colors that would suit either a boy or a girl. A yellow baby bed. A yellow chifforobe. A light orange carpet. I made orange-checkered curtains for the big window in the baby's room, and a matching quilt. I set a wind-up teddy bear on the pillow. By the time Ryan was born, that room was just beautiful.

I was a big woman, and healthy, and I was sure I wouldn't have any trouble. But then, when my time came, something seemed to go wrong. I was in labor for almost twenty-three hours. And after I delivered Ryan, on December 6, 1971, the pain didn't stop. I felt like I was still in labor. I kept calling the nurse. She told me to stop acting like a big baby. They brought Ryan to me. I wanted that little boy more than anything, but I was in so much pain I couldn't even hold him, and asked the nurse to take him away.

The lady next to me, who had two other kids, told me: "You're not supposed to be hurting so bad. You're not supposed to bleed like that."

The doctor came and pushed on my stomach. Blood clots came out. It was horrible; blood was everywhere. I lost consciousness. A specialist arrived.

"Wake up!" he yelled. "Jeanne, wake up, you can't fall asleep! Talk to me!"

"I'm tired."

"You have to stay awake!"

"Don't be mad at me," I said. "I'm just so tired . . ."

They sent helicopters all over Indiana to bring back Rh-negative blood for me. Thirteen pints of blood. I can remember looking around the room and seeing Mom and Dad, Wayne and the minister. I thought it was over, that I wasn't going to make it. I saw the tunnel that they talk about, and the light, just like my own mother had. But I never entered the tunnel either. I'd sort of dream about my little baby boy and think: *You can't die, because you have this baby now. You have to make it. For him.* That's what kept me fighting.

When I was finally out of danger, they brought Ryan back to me. I don't think I really understood that I had survived the ordeal until I held my baby in my arms. He was a cute little thing with a lot of hair. Dr. Fields asked if they could circumcise him. I said okay and kissed him and let them take him away and waited for them to bring him back to me again.

But they didn't.

"Where's my baby?"

"He's still bleeding from the circumcision, Jeanne."

"But why?"

"We're not sure. We've tried everything. We've put some

stitches in him, left his diaper off; we're using all kinds of ointments to try to get the bleeding stopped."

After three days, Ryan was still bleeding. Wayne and my folks took him to Methodist Hospital in Indianapolis to see the hematologist there. I was discharged and sent home. Since I was still too sick to get out of bed, I couldn't go with Mom and Wayne and waited alone to hear from them. But the hematologist at Methodist Hospital decided to call me before he spoke to them.

He was so straightforward, pulled no punches. He sounded like he was reading a script. He said: "Your son, Ryan White, has just been diagnosed with classic hemophilia. That means his blood does not clot. He has less than one percent clotting ability. There are different degrees of hemophilia and your son's is severe. You will have to be very cautious. He will never be able to play contact sports. He will never be able to have any major surgeries. If he is in a car accident, the chances of him surviving are almost zero because he will bleed faster than they can ever put blood into him."

Then he said, in an equally deadpan voice: "Hemophiliacs used to have to have blood transfusions, one after another. They would often die or be crippled by the time they were teens. Now we are very fortunate that we have this clotting factor which is just being approved by the Food and Drug Administration. The clotting factor is much easier to give. However, it has to be given in the hospital. So your son will probably require a lot of hospital stays.

"He'll be able to come home in a few days. Don't be alarmed when you see him. We had to give him a Mohawk haircut. He's had some IVs in the veins in his head."

And then he said good-bye and hung up.

I remember trying to take it all in. I remember thinking that the doctor was a horrid person because he didn't do anything to cushion the blow.

I thought: *My poor baby! He's got tubes hanging out of his head!* But it wasn't like that. The veins in a baby's head are always very pronounced, so they're the best veins on which to conduct blood tests. When Mom and Dad and Wayne brought him home, Ryan had twenty-one little pinholes in his head where they had stuck him.

How could this have happened? My little son had been born with a disease occurring only in boys and caused by a deformed gene carried by their mothers. It had a history of affecting the sons of European royalty. Half the cases were hereditary. But my mom and my grandma tested negative for the gene; I tested positive. So in our case, as in about half the cases, the gene just showed up out of the blue, without any inherited tendency.

It looked like my little Ryan had simply been unlucky. In this, he was exactly like about twenty thousand other American men.

When they tell you that something is terribly wrong with your child, it takes a while to be able to think clearly about it.

Ryan was born tall, twenty-two and a half inches long. He was real skinny—only 7.8 pounds—with big feet. I looked at this long, thin baby and thought with joy, like a real Indiana sports fan: I got my basketball player!

Then, when he was diagnosed with hemophilia, I thought: Well, there goes my basketball player.

And then I thought: Well, it doesn't matter. He can be something else.

If I ever felt disappointed, I was ashamed of myself and smashed down that unworthy feeling. Sure, I wanted a perfectly healthy child. Everybody does. But all through life, things come out not perfect. Even if people are born perfect, they eventually may not have perfect lives. So you have to say to yourself: It's the person inside that counts.

Look at all the people who can't have kids at all, I said to myself. Think how much luckier you are than they! I kept remembering one of Grandma Helen's sayings: "I wept that I had no shoes, until I met a man who had no feet."

When I would go into the hospital with Ryan and see some of those other children and what they had to contend with, I just said: Lord, thanks for giving me something I can really deal with that does not exceed my strength to handle it.

When we got through our initial panic and hysteria, we sat down and listened to the doctors. They told us that Factor VIII, the clotting factor, would help to make Ryan's hemophilia a controllable chronic disorder. It was expensive—$350 per shot. Ryan received up to two a week. However, we were factory workers, thank Heaven, and we had insurance.

I learned quickly that stories from other sufferers were often every bit as important as advice from your doctor. My family and I developed the habit of gathering intelligence in waiting rooms, at fund-raisers, on line at pharmacies.

Some folks said: "You have to pad the crib." Other folks said: "Make sure he always wears a football helmet." The great danger was not only that the child would cut himself but that he would bruise himself. Any bump could trigger a bleed internally, in a joint, that would cause terrible pain and swelling. Ryan would later explain that it was like pouring a quart of milk into a pint-size container, with no place for the excess to spill out. There was nothing to be done for it except to treat the pain and wait for the blood to dissipate. Meanwhile, every bleed would cause the child to have ugly external black-and-blue bruises. The parents of hemophiliacs often ran the risk of being suspected of child abuse for that reason.

One day a nice woman came to visit me. She brought her son, who was seven or eight at the time and a hemophiliac. One of his legs was already an inch shorter than the other because of so many hemorrhages in the knees. But he was a good-looking, cheerful boy and the sight of him filled me with hope that my little boy would grow strong despite the disease. In addition, this lady had another child, also a boy, and he *didn't* have the disease. I had planned never to have any more children . . . but when I heard that, I thought: *Well, maybe . . .*

My visitor said: "Every case is different. You'll just have to see what he can do and what he can't do. You'll learn by experience."

She was right. I quickly learned that Ryan couldn't be running around with the football helmet. That was only going to teach him to feel like he was sickly. And I didn't want that. I saw that handling this thing was very much a matter of attitude. I tried to make him see that different people are born with different things wrong with them, and you just have to learn to deal with what's wrong with you, and that's all there is to that. I wanted Ryan to think: *Yes, I've got a problem, but it's not going to ruin my life. I can do just about anything anybody else can do.*

I know that Ryan's positive attitude spilled over to help him when he had to deal with AIDS.

I told him: "Now, Ryan, when you start to feel a tingling sensation and you think you're getting a bleed, you come and tell Mom and we'll get you to the hospital and give you some Factor and then it won't hurt so much."

He soon began to take an active role in handling his illness.

Of course, they had advised me not to have another baby, and I had tried not to get pregnant. Still, accidents do happen. I was scared when they told me I was pregnant the second time. But deep down, I was thrilled. I felt it was a blessing. For some reason, I just knew the baby was going to be a girl. I had a lot of faith and thought the Lord wouldn't give me another hemophiliac. Wayne was furious when he heard that I was pregnant. But I told him while we were at work, so he couldn't make a real big scene.

Andrea was born on October 15, 1973. She arrived in maybe an hour and a half. No bleeding. No problems. What a beautiful baby she was! She was healthy and robust, with lots of hair. Right after she was born, I had my tubes tied . . . because I was so grateful to God for this blessing and afraid to test the generosity of fate any further.

I can remember Mom bringing Ryan to the hospital. They wouldn't let such a little child come up. I looked down from my third-floor-room window. He was standing on the hospital grounds waving up at me, with this big grin on his little face. He was two years old.

I said to myself: *Jeanne, your boy was born in the era of Factor VIII; your second child is a healthy girl; you are the luckiest woman in the world.*

When he was very young—four or five months; he wasn't even crawling yet—Ryan climbed up over the side of the crib. We found him sitting on the floor, laughing. By nine months he was walking. Before you knew it, he was potty trained. A thrill went through my heart. I realized I had a real smart kid.

Maybe because he had to limit his physical activity so much, Ryan became a really fascinated reader. He loved Dr. Seuss and The Berenstein Bears. When he was ten years old, his grandparents asked him what he wanted for Christmas, and he said, "A subscription to *Time* magazine."

We accepted him as our smart kid. He always knew just a little bit more than the rest of us.

Ryan frequently had to go to the hospital, and whenever he did, I went with him and stayed with him. At Riley Hospital, they always let parents stay. But at other hospitals, the nurses hated that.

"It's hospital policy. Parents can't stay."

"Dr. Fields said that I could stay."

"He didn't leave any orders."

"Then it must have been an oversight. I'm staying anyway."

"Mrs. White!"

"Please don't be mad at me. But that's just the way it is."

Our trips to the emergency room were like a recurring nightmare of unceasing ignorance and incompetence.

Once, Ryan was hanging on the towel bar in the bathroom and it came right out of the wall. He had padding on his joints that time, but as luck would have it, he hit his head and needed five stitches. The emergency-room personnel gave him Factor VIII and sent him home with his head all wrapped up with gauze. He didn't want to sleep in his own bed after that, so we took him into bed with us.

I woke up in the middle of the night, feeling that my gown was wet. I thought maybe Ryan had peed in bed, but he never did that. I reached to pull my gown away from my body and felt this real thick gooey stuff. I screamed and jumped up out of bed and turned on the light. Sure enough, the whole bed, me, Wayne, Ryan, we were all covered in blood. If Ryan had been in his own bed that night, he would have bled to death. From then on I knew that he could never just be treated and discharged. Any injury would require a hospital stay.

One Christmas Eve when he was about five, we were at Mom and Dad's, and Ryan started to run a real high fever. The doctor said I should take him to the emergency room. But before he arrived to supervise, the nurses had given Ryan a shot to lower his fever.

"Wait a minute!" I cried. "You shouldn't be doing that! This boy's a hemophiliac and he's going to have to have the Factor if you give him a shot."

"Don't worry, Ms. White. We used a very small needle. He'll be fine."

They sent him home. His hip hemorrhaged and swelled up like a giant boil. He was in agony for three days.

The experience of living with Ryan's hemophilia put me in constant conflict with my own natural personality. I was a shy woman, a docile person, used to taking orders, taking care, making things nice. And here, these ignorant, obstinate medical people were turning me into an aggressive, pushy mother who could create a big stink right out in public. I was quickly learning: Doctors and nurses are not gods. They don't always know the truth. They don't always *tell* the truth.

It was bad enough that there were nurses who wouldn't listen to me; some of them wouldn't even listen to the child. I remember, when Ryan was about six, he had a hemorrhage in his kidneys and couldn't urinate. It was terrible. He was crying, miserable.

In the hospital, he kept saying he was going to vomit. But this grumpy, mean nurse kept telling him he was not going to do any such thing. I asked her to let me take him, but she refused and said he had to come with her to the examining room. When she went to pick him up, Ryan vomited all over her. I thought: *He tried to tell you.* Then something released in his kidneys and he urinated everywhere. She was fit to be tied.

"Now I've got to go change my uniform!" she hollered.

I was so happy that he was finally peeing again that I think I actually laughed. I thought: *Lady, your uniform is the last of my worries.*

My strength with these medical people came gradually. I knew there was going to be nobody to speak out for my child but me. Ryan had confidence in me. He'd say to people: "My mom can treat my hemophilia. She knows how better than anybody."

I made my share of mistakes with Ryan, and I remember every single one of them with the same aching guilt that I felt at the time. He was always a collector, even as a little kid. The matchbox cars were his treasure. He always took six or eight to bed with him, as many as he could handle. Every night I would go in and get all the cars out of his bed after he went to sleep. One night I missed one. He rolled over on it, and the next morning his whole neck had hemorrhaged. I wept and berated myself. Guilt left me sleepless.

Until Ryan was three, if he had a bleeding episode, I had to take him to the hospital so they could give him the Factor in an IV. When I heard about a program that would enable him to receive it in the doctor's office, I jumped at it. We went on Mondays and Thursdays to get Factor VIII, so he would be okay over the weekend. Wayne never came with us. When Ryan was five, the doctors suggested that I try giving the Factor myself. I thought: *No! I'm not smart enough to give shots!* Then I thought: *If these nurses can learn to do it, why can't I?* It took me three months of training, but I learned. It would have made our lives a lot easier if Wayne had learned as well. He didn't. He just didn't want to be involved with Ryan's illness.

We kept the Factor in our refrigerator. I'd pick up eight to twelve boxes at a time from Riley Hospital and mix up the injection as I needed it. If Ryan was going to stay overnight someplace, we'd give him the Factor as a prophylactic, to protect him in case something happened. Tom, my dad, was the most cautious one in our family when it came to Ryan. He had heard a rumor, from someone at Riley or someone at the pharmacy, that the more you took the

Factor, the more likely you were to develop an inhibitor reaction which would make it less and less effective as time went by.

"I don't like that Factor," Dad said with a suspicious frown. "You're giving him too much of that stuff."

I didn't see that we had an alternative.

Ryan eventually began to take care of himself quite a bit. He learned what he could do and could not do. But he wanted to do it all. We were real leery about having him ride a bike and made him wear knee pads. Once he learned, he tossed them away.

He tried Little League. I'd tell the coaches everything about his disease so that they wouldn't be scared and would know what to do if something happened. But during practice one day, he was hit in the mouth by a fly ball and started bleeding. The coach handled it fine. He called me and I gave Ryan some of the Factor. After that, however, Ryan didn't want to play anymore. He had matured enough to know fear. He always missed baseball—not so much the game itself but the social aspects of being part of the team. He still loved the game—he just couldn't play it.

Ryan could always tell when a bleed was coming on. His skin tingled. And then, slowly, the vessels underneath would start swelling with blood. As soon as he felt a bleed beginning, we could give him the Factor and the bleed would stop. But as he got older, he set his own agenda. If he thought the bleed and its treatment would keep him from doing something he really wanted to do, he wouldn't tell me about it. I'd get real mad when he did that. Because then it would get really bad and he'd have to go the hospital and it would take two or three or four days for the swelling to dissipate.

He was always supposed to wear Ace bandages when he had a bleed. Often he ignored that rule. The doctors would say: "He needs to be on crutches for the next three or four days." But Ryan would never use the crutches. He would try to walk as normally as possible. He didn't like kids saying: "What's wrong with you now?"

He got used to being in the hospital two or three times a month, to receive the Factor after a minor scrape or bruise. Riley Hospital became his home away from home.

"I saw this kid who was burned, Mom. He spilled something hot on himself and got all burned up, his whole face and chest and arms. He was in such pain . . . I saw this kid with cancer. He's getting chemotherapy and he has no hair and he vomits all the time . . . I saw these kids who are so retarded, they have to wear diapers and they're in their teens. . . ."

"Oh, honey, I hate for you to be with such sick children, to see so much suffering."

"It's okay, Mom. I'm just glad all that's wrong with me is my hemophilia."

I do believe that evil befalls folks who do evil, that what goes around comes around. But I never felt that Ryan's disease was a punishment. Never. I always felt like I had tried to live a decent, good life and that, for that reason, I would not have received such a punishment, and furthermore, that the Lord would never have afflicted an innocent little boy in order to teach me a lesson.

No, this illness of Ryan's felt to me much more like a test than a punishment. We all get tested in this life. God gives you tests to see how you can handle them. I always thought: I am going to handle this test, Lord. You will see.

I felt that handling the tests that life brought was how you worked your way to Heaven.

Chapter 2

"Let's just pretend I don't have it."

An illness in the family belongs to everybody in the family. You can't escape it. Even if you're not the main caregiver, even if you never change a bandage or carry a bedpan or drive a suffering child to the hospital, that illness will invade your life and haunt you. Better to face the illness and do battle with it directly than to try to avoid it—because that's the only way you have a chance of winning the battle.

I often think if my husband had shared in caring for Ryan, then Ryan's illness wouldn't have felt like such a mystery and a threat to him, and would not have depressed him so.

The center of our social life was the euchre club, six or eight couples who would gather—each week at a different house—to play cards and have a few laughs. One of the guys who played euchre with us was always trying to get Wayne to go out drinking with him. After Ryan was born, he began to succeed.

Wayne had never been a drinker. I hardly noticed when he began drinking beer, or hard liquor. Only when I saw him acting kind of silly did I ask myself: *Is he drunk?* It didn't seem possible. It seemed you should have to drink more to be drunk.

Wayne was a joker; he'd do anything for a laugh. He always embarrassed people. If somebody's stomach rumbled, or somebody spilled a drink, he would go on and on forever about it and get everybody laughing at the person. He'd humiliate me constantly because of my weight. If I ate something, he'd say—in front of everybody—"You don't need that!" I'd feel myself turning scarlet and run to the kitchen to hide. If you answered Wayne in kind, told him he was skinny or that his jokes weren't funny, he'd get mad. When he started drinking, he'd get mean.

With Ryan, he always seemed to play too hard. He'd lift him by the hands or by the head and hold him up in the air.

"That hurts, Dad!" Ryan would cry.

"Oh, no, it doesn't," Wayne would say. "You're just a big sissy."

Ryan would feel embarrassed and fight back the tears. When he got older, he never talked about his illness with Wayne. He sensed that Wayne had a hard time dealing with the hemophilia—and he tried to spare him having any part of it.

I felt if I could get Wayne away from his drinking buddies, he would be transformed. Our original attraction for each other would return; the growing sickness in our marriage would go into remission. We had a wonderful time on vacation to Florida when Ryan was five and Andrea was three. Then as soon as we came home, Wayne was out every night again, and most of the time he'd come home drunk.

Truthfully, I didn't miss him. I was even glad to be rid of him because we had begun to fight so much, and I didn't want the kids to be around that. It seemed like I was always on him about something. I tried to stop myself. I learned what to say and when to let things drop, just not to make him mad, just not to have Ryan and Andrea listening while we tore each other apart.

Wayne had never struck me when he was sober. Now he occasionally gave me a swat, and I couldn't stand for that. One night he shoved me so that I fell between these two stools. He stood there laughing while I floundered and flopped, trying to get up. When I finally regained my footing, I punched him in the stomach. He staggered back, hurt.

"You're not going to do that to me," I said. "You're not going to start beating me up. It will not happen." I shoved him away and shut myself in the bedroom. He never raised a hand to me again after that.

When Ryan was about five, Wayne announced that he and a drinking buddy were taking their boys fishing. I was pleased; I thought that would be fun for the kids. But it turned out not to be a fishing trip like the ones we used to have up at Lake Bruce with Dad. This was one of those fishing trips where the men sit around the campfire boozing and the boys watch.

On the way home Wayne was so smashed that he ran right into some guy's fence. When the guy came out of his house yelling, Wayne fled to our house—and ran right into the wall of the garage. With Ryan in the car! I went crazy.

"Look at you! You're totally smashed! You could have killed this child!"

"Aw, leave me alone . . ."

"You're a drunk, Wayne. You've got to get help."

"I am not a drunk. I am fine. I can take it or leave it."

"You've got a problem!"

"*You've* got the problem, Jeanne. Why don't you go on a diet?!"

That really got to me. The biggest hang-up in my life has always been my weight. I'd think: *Lord, why, why, why did You make me heavy?* Then I'd think: *If I wasn't heavy, who knows what type of person I might have been? If I had a gorgeous body, big boobs and little hips, who knows, I might have been a stripper!*

But you can't make fun of your own hang-ups unless you're feeling real strong. And right at that moment, faced with an angry, drunken husband and a crumbling marriage, I didn't feel strong at all. I responded to Wayne's counterattack by going on a killer diet.

Everybody thought I looked terrific at one hundred and forty pounds.

Everybody thought I looked sick at one hundred and sixteen pounds. It turned out I was. I had this terrible burning feeling in my lungs. It was impossible to inhale. They put me in the hospital, convinced that I had lung cancer, and told me that I had to stop smoking. I kept telling everybody: "I never smoked in my life!" But they insisted on showing me these horrible pictures of lungs which had been destroyed by tobacco smoke. Finally they put me in the Indiana University Medical Center and ran some more tests.

Wayne came to see me. He was drunk and upset about some bill he thought I had not paid. Nothing I could say would stop him from calling me names and yelling. The hospital staff stood gaping; the lady in the bed next to me was horrified. For the first time, I really saw Wayne through the eyes of other people, and I thought to myself: *Jeanne, you are not going to live like this. You have a good job, two wonderful kids, a supportive family who will stand by you; there is no reason to go on subjecting yourself and your children to this kind of abuse. If you have to be Mom and Dad both, then so be it. Your children deserve a home like you had. A loving home.*

I made myself a promise that if I got out of this hospital and didn't have lung cancer, I was going to divorce Wayne White.

The tests came back negative. I didn't have cancer; I had a lymph node infection called sarcoidosis. It's serious; some folks can die from it. But if you're lucky, as I was, you get rid of it with rest and antibiotics.

I had Wayne served with divorce papers while he was at work—because, as with the announcement of my second pregnancy, I was scared of his reaction. I also dared to hope he might be happy about the separation. Instead, he turned up all tearful and begged me to stay with him. He said he would stop drinking, go to church again; anything I wanted. I think he panicked at the idea of losing the security of a home and kids and a wife.

He said, "I'll stay with my mom for a few days, and then we'll see, okay?"

"Sure," I answered. But I knew there was no way I was going back with him.

Wayne was convinced I must have a lover. He went over to my parents' house and my brother's house and insisted I was cheating on him. He was wrong. I had no lover. What I did have was a wonderful friend named Steve Ford.

Steve had taken over my job when I became ill. He struck up a real close friendship with Barb Dukes, who worked on the line next to me and was also a good friend of mine. When I returned and took back my old job, she got us acquainted. Steve moved into another job elsewhere in Delco, but we became friends and started dating.

Steve was quite a bit older than I was. He was a group leader and a UAW representative. He had been married several times but had no children. Maybe Steve and I shouldn't have married. However, each of us needed something from the other right then. I wanted a father for my children and he wanted a family.

One evening, after the divorce proceedings had already been started, Wayne came in the house drunk, saw me in the living room talking with Steve, went totally crazy and pulled a gun. Of course, I didn't think it was actually loaded. "Now see here, Wayne," I said, "you just put that foolish thing away right this minute." Only afterwards did I discover that gun *was* loaded.

I filed around the first of June. We were divorced in September. Steve Ford and I got married September 30 in a little church in Gatlinburg, Tennessee. Nobody we knew was there.

I sold the house that I had lived in with Wayne and split the proceeds with him. Then I pooled my money with Steve Ford and we built a new house on two acres on Route 213 in Windfall, over where Steve's folks and his brother and sister lived. I loved those people. They were a great family. I loved the woods at the back of the yard and the feeling of space under the wide Indiana sky. I canned corn and peas and green beans that we had grown in our own garden. I even put up beef stew and chili.

When I married Steve, Ryan was seven and Andrea was five. She had been a perfect baby. She ate everything without complaint; she slept through the night from the start. You put her down for a nap and she would not stir until two hours later. She adored Ryan and wanted to do everything he did. He played with her all the time. She was his cuddly puppet. He could bounce her, chase her, put rice pudding in her hair, and she'd just giggle and coo. When he had to go in the hospital, she'd wave bye-bye to us without a problem and cuddle up in my mother's arms and wait patiently for our return.

I had a ball making clothes for her. Bell-bottoms. Jumpsuits. Little sundresses with matching panties with ruffles on them. But she was a real tomboy and wanted to be just like her brother. Ryan showed her how to build whole towns out of Lego; he taught her how to put everything away neatly, each little plane into its little hangar, each little car into its little box. To our dismay, Andrea showed absolutely no inclination to put anything away herself, and when she was about four years old, she abandoned her dolls and her pretty clothes in favor of T-shirts and jeans and went out to play in the mud. She was a real tomboy. She would run as fast and throw as far as any kid on our block.

One day, right after Steve and I were married, we heard that Delco was offering afternoon roller-skating at the local rink. It was close to the house, so we figured we'd take the kids over there after work. The very first time Andrea went out on that floor, she could skate. She went around a couple of times with Ryan guiding her and then *whoosh!* she took off. Ryan, Steve and I stood there amazed, watching her race around that rink, shouting, "Hi! Look at me!" as she passed us in a blur of blond hair and rosy cheeks.

"Can I have lessons, Mom?" she pleaded. "I want to learn to skate backwards and everything. I want to be really good. Can I have lessons?"

The first teacher I asked turned me down because he thought

she wasn't good enough yet. That got me into a big huff. By my standards—I could barely stay upright on skates—Andrea was a whiz. I asked another teacher, Rick Gunning, who had just started a skating club. He took one look at her and said he would be delighted to take her on.

Roller-skating is judged in the same way as ice-skating, except that the sport is much harder because of the weight of the skates. It's too bad that it still doesn't qualify as an Olympic event. It really should. There's a double mapes, which is the same as a double toe loop on ice. There are spins, jumps and double loops and double salchows. Roller skaters now do triple jumps, just as they do on ice.

The club had about eight members. Andrea was the youngest. She improved very fast. In no time flat she could do a set spin and then come up. After her first year of skating, she qualified for a big state meet. My mom made her a costume with a big butterfly on it. She placed third. They gave her a trophy. I just about fainted with pride.

Steve Ford loved the skating. On Sundays he'd take both kids to the rink and skate with them himself. He said we should spare no expense to keep Andrea involved and to train her and outfit her.

We heard about a terrific teacher in Alexandria, Indiana, named Jim Harmer. The members of his skating club came from all over the Midwest, and often made it to the national competitions. When Andrea joined Harmer's club, she met other skaters her own age, and I was real pleased by that. But the schedule became very hectic. She practiced every night after school and Saturday mornings from 6 A.M. until noon. There were times when we stayed in Alexandria all day Saturday. I'd get back at eight o'clock at night; we'd have supper and fall into bed and go back and spend all day Sunday.

In her first year with Jim Harmer, Andrea won the state meet in the primary division. Then she placed third in the regionals, which included skaters from Wisconsin, Michigan, Indiana, Ohio and Illinois. That meant that she qualified to go to the nationals. And she had been skating for only *two years!* The teacher who had refused to take her on admitted it was a big mistake. Her first teacher—who had hoped she would be *his* champion—was real upset with us for leaving.

Andrea was a powerful, clean skater with wonderful lines. Her big problem was the amount of time she had to dedicate to practice. She wanted to play on teams at school: softball, basketball. And she couldn't, because every free minute went to skating.

All the other skaters were nervous wrecks before a meet, psyching themselves up with motivational tapes that said, "You're the best you can win go go go!" Not my Andrea. She said, "If I do good, I do good. If I don't, I don't." She had a highly developed sense of reality. "If I skate really well, Mom, I think I might make third."

Her attitude suited me. I didn't want to tell her she was the best in the world and have her go out and think she could beat all those girls and then come back in last place. I wanted her to be aware that other children were good skaters, too. If they hit their double loop or their double salchow and she didn't hit hers just as perfectly, then she wasn't going to place, and she had to know that could happen and that it was okay.

Andrea's favorite event was free-style—although she also competed in figures, dance and pairs. Sometimes she'd fall so hard that you thought surely she'd be hurt. But then she'd get right back up and do it over and over.

She had a seven-jump combination—axel, loop, double mapes, loop, double mapes, uller, double flip—that was just terrific. She had a wonderful "Broken Ankle" (where she'd spin on the sides of her wheels) and inverted spin. If she hit those moves, she was unbeatable.

A friend of mine from high school, Susan Slaughter, made Andrea's basic costumes, and then I added the glitter. Sequins, bugle beads, aurora stones, which give off all the colors of the rainbow—each tiny stone had to be attached separately. It was worth all the effort to see your child shining.

I loved getting to know the other mothers and kids in the skating club. We'd have great times together. Jackie Vollenhaus, Linda Sample, Ann Drew, Linda Kays, Faye Barrett, Luci Buck, Sherri Keston—they were the best skating mothers in the whole world and remained my friends through everything. We shared rooms at nationals to cut costs. Sometimes we stayed three in a room and the kids slept on the floor.

For the first time, in that skating club, we met men who were openly gay. They were friendly. They did not act different from other men. Their private lives were private. The mothers and the kids were friends with them, and skated with them. In an easy, day-to-day way, Andrea's extraordinary athletic ability had expanded the size of my world.

In 1983, Steve and I divorced very amicably. Our marriage may not have worked, but it had warmth and respect and fun and a lot of comfort. For my beautiful little towheaded daughter, it was the best thing I ever did—because it gave her a real father. Steve was crazy about Andrea. Even after we were divorced, he always went to see her at nationals.

I moved back to Kokomo, to a little house on Webster Street, to be near my mom and dad.

Andrea transferred to Melody Skateland, Indianapolis, where

Larry Dorset, and his wife, Karen Mejia, both champion skaters, became her teachers. She found a pairs partner, and she started doing free dance. That year, 1984, she made it to nationals in three events. She placed fourth in Juvenile Girls' Singles, second in Juvenile Dance with Scott Eller. She made the finals in pairs with her partner, Darren Merkle. She was runner-up for the Harmer Trophy, the Indiana Skater of the Year award.

Maybe Andrea grew to champion level in reaction to Ryan's not being able to do anything athletic. (Maybe she just takes after my athletic sister, Janet.) I don't know. I never thought about the psychological background of her prowess. I just felt that skating was something that she could do naturally, and if she wanted to compete for the championship, then I was determined to encourage her. Anyone who is that coordinated, that strong and motivated, should be supported.

At nationals, we met a boy named Mike Underwood, a terrific skater. He and Andrea hit it off and decided they'd like to compete as partners. I took her to Chicago to try out with him, and they were adorable together. By the end of August 1984, we had begun driving every weekend to Chicago so Andrea could skate with Mike. For two months we kept up this pace. Finally it was getting to be impossible to do it anymore. To make it easier on me, Mike's thoughtful parents started meeting us halfway in Rensselaer at a truck stop. They'd pick up Andrea and take her back with them and keep her all weekend. I would return on Sunday and pick her up.

Ryan came with me three or four times, but he was really bored watching his sister and Mike practice. He seemed listless, distracted. I'd leave him with my folks and when I returned from my long drive, I'd find him lying around the house, not asleep, but not doing anything. It wasn't like him.

The next weekend, I headed west with an uneasy mind. I thought to myself: *You work all week, Jeanne. You spend all this extra money driving all these miles all weekend. Monday morning you're back at work. Andrea does nothing but skate. You hardly ever see Ryan. Maybe this is not such a great arrangement.*

One weekend, Andrea and I were driving home and we hit a terrible rainstorm. I squinted through the beating wipers, trying to see the edges of the road and not lose sight of the car crawling along ahead of me.

"Andrea hon, if we get home, this is going to have to stop. I just can't hardly handle this schedule anymore. Ryan's not feeling good, and here we are in this storm, and I have no idea how he's doing. What if we had an accident in a storm like this and Ryan was left all alone?"

"I understand, Mom."

We made it back to Kokomo. I drove straight to my mother's house. Ryan was very sick.

He'd get a little better; then he'd get sick again. He ran fevers. Then they'd go away. He woke up in the middle of the night sweating. His stomach hurt him. He had diarrhea. His lymph nodes were swollen. The doctors gave him antibiotics.

Mike Underwood and his folks were wonderful. They kept Andrea for one whole weekend after another while Ryan's baffled doctors tried to figure out what was wrong.

In November 1984, Ryan went to the clinic at which all the local hemophiliacs had their annual screening of blood work. The clinic was important as a check to make sure you weren't building up inhibitors, that the Factor was still working as it should. Ryan hated clinics because they were so boring. Blood tests. Dental exams.

Questions. At this clinic, he tested positive for hepatitis B. The doctors asked me if he had been sick a lot during the past year, and I said, "Yes," thinking it must have been because of the hepatitis.

We were told that we were going to be receiving a new, heat-treated factor that would be a lot safer than the old stuff. The label on the new factor said something about a less-than-one-percent chance of AIDS. We had heard of AIDS in homosexuals, of course. The only hemophiliacs whom we had heard of who had contracted the terrifying new disease were supposedly older men who had received blood transfusions before Factor VIII became available. The Factor itself had never before been questioned in this regard.

At the end of that clinic visit, I had supplies of both heat-treated and non–heat-treated factors in my refrigerator. Nobody told us to stop using the non–heat-treated factor. Just a few days later, Ryan got sick.

On December 6, 1984, Ryan turned thirteen years old. The next day, he got off the school bus, came into the house and said, "Mom, you've got to do something. I can't even get off the school bus without being tired. I can't figure out what's wrong. We had to run a lap today and I couldn't do it and the teacher got real upset with me."

That weekend, he ran a fever of one hundred and four. Our doctors said to give him Tylenol, but the fever wouldn't go down. On Monday morning, when Ryan wasn't any better, I took him over to the doctors' office. They put him in the hospital and sent him right up for X-rays and asked me to wait for the results.

The X-rays showed that he had pneumonia in both lungs. They admitted him. They gave him all kinds of antibiotics. The attendants pounded his chest and his back. It hurt so bad, he couldn't stand it.

"Ryan, you've got to cough it up," they said. "You've got to get that stuff out of your chest. You're not trying to get better."

And he said to me, "Mom, there is nothing to come up. They keep telling me I'm not cooperating, but there is nothing to cough up. Why can't they understand that?"

Dr. Fields walked me down the hall. I had known him for years and years. I could read every tone, every gesture . . . and I knew he was frightened.

"The antibiotics are not working," he said. "Ryan should be getting better by now. We're going to transfer him to Riley Hospital for Children. We're taking him in an ambulance, because he needs oxygen."

I kept hearing my Dad's voice saying: *I don't like that Factor. You're giving him too much of that stuff.*

I kept hearing the voice of the attendant at the hemophilia clinic. *This is the new, heat-treated Factor. It's much safer than the old kind.*

Suddenly I turned to the head nurse. "Did the doctor say anything about AIDS?" I asked. Her face registered shock, then suspicion, then rejection.

"Oh, no, they didn't say anything about anything like that," she responded.

I put the nurse's reactions out of my mind, and went with Mom and Andrea to Indianapolis. At Riley, they had Ryan in the emergency room with so many specialists around him that Andrea and I could barely get in to see him. He looked so worn out. He couldn't breathe without the oxygen. His eyes brimmed with questions no one could answer: *What's wrong with me, Mom? What's going on? Tell me! Help me!*

All I could say was: "You rest, hon. You're going to be all right."

The doctor who talked to me was a man I had never met before—Martin Kleiman, an expert on infectious diseases in children.

"Ryan doesn't have bacterial pneumonia," he said. "We know because the antibiotics would have worked on that. We can find out whether he has TB real fast. There's always the possibility of cancer, too. But first we have to find out what kind of pneumonia he has. And for that, we need to take a biopsy of his lungs. Before we can do the surgery, we need to bring up his clotting level. So we have to give him the Factor. We need you to sign a permission slip, because there is a possibility that complications could arise during surgery."

I signed the papers.

I know now that Dr. Kleiman considered that it might be AIDS the minute he heard Dr. Fields describe Ryan's case on the phone. It was Ryan's hemophilia that made him suspect. He had seen a lot of children with pneumonia caused by Pneumocystis carinii. It was a microbe that lived as a parasite in people and in many animals. Usually it didn't cause any trouble. But when the immune system was compromised, either because of disease or drugs used to treat disease, then it could cause a kind of viral pneumonia characterized by a hard, dry, constant cough and an eventual breakdown of lung function. You could tell when somebody's immune system had deteriorated, because there was a huge decline in the number of T lymphocyte cells in the person's blood. These were calls that we learned about in high school biology as the white antibodies that naturally fight off infection. In the era of AIDS, they are called T cells. Dr. Kleiman's experience with pneumocystis was in children who had leukemia, or tumors which destroyed the T cells or required chemotherapy that blew out the immune system. These kids usually looked kind of yellowish because of the liver involvement. But when he heard Dr. Fields's description of Ryan, whose major symptom was not yellowness but paralyzing weakness, he thought there might be some possibility that this child who was coming in had the dreaded new disease, AIDS.

I waited with Andrea for the surgery to be over, honestly half hoping it would turn out to be cancer, because I had seen so many kids with cancer cured at Riley. In a couple of hours, Dr. Kleiman returned.

"We've done the biopsy and Ryan's okay. It looks like he's got a viral pneumonia."

I didn't know what that meant.

"We're sending the biopsy to Denver for a reading . . ."

I waited. My mind went blank. I didn't pray. I held my daughter's hand. At about two in the morning on December 18, Dr. Kleiman told us that the biopsy had come back and had revealed that Ryan had pneumocystis, which meant he had full-blown AIDS.

I remember thinking: There's no way I would want to live if something happens to my son. My life without one of my children would be too empty.

I could not imagine losing my child. I could not believe that he really had AIDS and would die. I thought: This is so new that maybe they don't quite know what they are dealing with. Maybe something else is creating results that look like AIDS. I'll make them run the tests over and maybe the results will come out differently.

I said to my eleven-year-old daughter, Andrea, "If this turns out to be true, and Ryan really does have AIDS and is going to die, I want us all to go together. We'll get in the car and turn on the engine and that'll be the end."

Andrea didn't say a word. She just held my hand and squeezed and let me talk and hugged me. Imagine, a little eleven-year-old girl having so much understanding. She says that she never thought that I meant it.

Later on, when they told us Ryan had three to six months to live, I thought to myself: How can I now face my daughter when I have said something so stupid to her?! As Ryan's life continued, and every day we thanked the Lord for another day, and another day, I saw the preciousness of life even more! I know that as a mother, I should never, ever have said that thing to my little girl. How must she have felt, to think that I was ready to forfeit my life and hers, to imagine that her life wasn't enough to make me want to go on living! How frightened she must have been! Just because her brother was sick, how could I have assumed she would want to give up her life? I was thinking about me and my emptiness and my loneliness without Ryan and all of us not being together, and I was not thinking about her and how special she was in my life.

I was so regretful that I had ever said those words; it just broke my heart.

When Ryan was home and feeling better, I said to her:

"Hon, you know what I said about us all getting in the car and turning it on and going together . . ."

And Andrea answered, "I don't remember that, Mom."

"You do, too . . ."

And she just gave me a big smile.

It was a perfect example of a child's infinite love and understanding.

I'll always be ashamed of that moment when I lost all hope and asked my daughter to commit suicide with me. It was a true feeling of mine, and I have to admit to it, but it didn't last long. When it passed I wanted to live even more; I wanted Ryan and Andrea to live even more.

I had no basis on which to comprehend the disease. Nothing made any sense to me. In minutes my family and I were living with words we had never heard before: "autoimmunity," "opportunistic." One treatment for pneumocystis was Septra, a sulfa drug, administered by painful shots in the leg. Ryan had an allergic reaction to it and nearly died.

He had tubes in his feet, in his legs, two tubes coming out of his chest, tubes in his nose, several in his mouth. They stuck another tube down in his lungs to suction him out. It was like watching some medieval torture—except that a mom doesn't ever really watch; she *feels*. I felt like this suffering would never end.

They put him on a respirator. That terrified me because I associated those machines with people who were in comas and would never recover. They told me he would be on the respirator for only a day or two; three days later, he was still on it. One tube created a real bad sore in the corner of his mouth. It looked terrible because of the way the hemophilia caused it to bleed under the skin. They kept him pretty well sedated and his eyes covered, but he was awake enough to mumble things into my ear when I leaned close to him, and to write me notes, asking to be suctioned out because he couldn't breathe.

Everything took so much longer than they said it would. They'd come by and look at him, and then say they would come by tomorrow. And I'd think: *Well, what if he can get the tube out in an hour or two, why should he have to wait until tomorrow?! Why can't you come back sooner?!* Even worse was that, if you stepped out at the wrong time, you might miss the doctor when he came by. You waited a whole day for those five minutes with the doctor.

That's the most frustrating thing about having a sick child in the hospital. You sit by his bed, you watch him, you know everything that's going on—and you have no influence on his treatment. For example, they'd come in and weigh Ryan when he had all those tubes in him. It was such a huge effort, to get the machine under him, to lift him up. And I wanted to scream: "Why don't you wait for a few days until the tubes are out?! Why are you putting him through so much pain?!"

Dr. Kleiman was calling everybody he could think of to consult about Ryan. The Centers for Disease Control in Atlanta (CDC). The National Institutes of Health (NIH). Medical centers in Canada. He gave Ryan a drug called pentamidine. It worked. The pneumonia began to clear out of my boy's lungs.

On December 22 they started removing the tubes. On the morning of the twenty-fourth, they took Ryan off the respirator. Then they took the patches off his eyes. He still had a tube in his throat and if he moved, it would make him cough and choke. So he tried hard not to move.

Years later, when my father had a heart attack and they put a similar tube down his throat, I remember Ryan leaning down over him, saying, "Now, Grandpa, don't you move, because if you do, it tickles and makes you want to cough."

There was no blood test available at that time to test for the presence of AIDS. So the CDC, which was trying to give support to physicians making diagnoses in the field, provided Riley with the serology testing so everyone around the patient—family members and medical professionals—could be easily tested for the presence of the virus. Dr. Kleiman gave me a questionnaire which he had received from a group of infection-control people doing a family contacts study. It had a long list of questions, from the most mundane—*Do you often share drinking glasses and eating utensils with your family members?*—to the most intimate—*Do you have anal sex? Do you have multiple sexual partners? Of which gender?*—and on and on.

I was terrified. *We're all going to get it!* I thought. I imagined Andrea and Mom and Dad with those tubes in their lungs, my brother and his family struggling for breath. "We're a real affectionate family," I cried hysterically to the official surveyors. "We hug! We kiss! We share drinks! We use each other's towels!"

They shook their heads and smiled. "No family member has ever come down with AIDS from ordinary household contact," they said. "You have nothing to worry about."

They were experts. I believed them. I held Andrea close to me and breathed easy. I answered all their questions, no matter how embarrassing. *Just stop it*, I thought. *Just cure it before my boy dies.*

Both Dr. Kleiman and I knew immediately that Ryan had contracted AIDS from his Factor. It sat at home in my refrigerator, a death sentence in a small blue and white box. We the users of the product had never had any idea where they went to get the blood to make the Factor.

I later learned that the pharmaceutical companies needed thousands and thousands of pints of blood, such a huge volume that they could never have depended on donations. They had to pay people for their blood. Naturally, some IV drug users slipped through and availed themselves of this chance to make some fast money for the next fix. All the blood would be in a big container; then the container would be spun real fast so that the clotting Factor was separated. That became the basis of our Factor.

What nobody realized then was that *one* infected donor could contaminate the whole batch. Ryan got at least two shots a week, and sometimes if he'd have a bleed, he'd get a shot every day for maybe thirty days. So he was probably infected not once but thousands of times.

Once I understood the procedure, I thought: *There's no way any hemophiliac could escape getting AIDS.* In the years since, I have heard of mild hemophiliacs who had only one shot of the Factor in their entire lives and who are HIV-infected. Only a few were not infected by the Factor and tests are now going on to find out why.

Suddenly, within a short time, Ryan was completely isolated. You couldn't go in to see him without wearing a gown and gloves. Laura Kreich, a wonderful young nurse, always volunteered to take care of Ryan if she was on duty. As far as I could see, the hospital staff was well informed and trained, and not particularly scared.

One day, however, Andrea and I were in the little snack area. A physician whom we had met was sitting nearby, talking to a nurse.

"I absolutely refuse to go in that kid's room," she said, "and you are not going to make me."

It took me some minutes to realize she was talking about Ryan.

The next hint of paranoia came when two of Ryan's teachers paid him a visit. They brought a lot of cards and letters from his classmates because he had by then missed so much school. And they asked me what was wrong with him.

"They say he has AIDS," I said, "but I really don't believe it. I think they'll find out that it's something else. Ryan will be very pleased to see you. You can take the cards and letters and go on in to see him yourself."

"No, that's all right," they said.

I said, "No, really, it's okay. All you have to do is put on the gown and gloves and you can go on in and see him."

They had this pained look on their faces. They said, "That's okay. We'll just leave the cards and letters here."

I thought: *My goodness, they look like they're scared of him.*

69

That was my first realization that maybe I shouldn't have told them.

People ask me all the time why we went public, and I tell them that we never went public, we just didn't know not to. We didn't know that people would treat Ryan like he had the plague. I mean, I thought everybody else knew more about AIDS than I did. It never dawned on me to lie to people. I didn't dream that people would think only gay men and IV drug users got it and that Ryan would have to be one of those to become infected. I thought that all I had to do was tell people he got it from his Factor, and they would believe me.

I can remember thinking: Is he really going to die? We don't know that for sure. They could have all kinds of things to cure this disease real soon. Especially with all these people coming down with it now, they're going to be looking harder and harder for a cure; surely they'll find one.

I said to myself: Jeanne, what you have to do now is believe. *This is the first time for you to prove your faith, to show the Lord that you believe in His healing.*

My brother encouraged me to believe in miracles. I had never seen anybody get a miracle, but I felt if I believed long enough and hard enough, then I would get a miracle for Ryan.

I didn't want to tell Ryan that he had AIDS, because that might make the Lord think I was doubting Him, and I knew if you doubt, you can cut yourself off from miracles. I kept having this vision that Ryan was going to wake up and be well, and all the doctors and nurses would come and say, "Gee, Mrs. White, we don't know what happened, it's just unbelievable, but somehow Ryan is cured."

All through the days before Christmas, I sat in the lobby with the other mothers of hospitalized children, keeping watch, thinking of all these children who needed a miracle. Riley personnel were trying to get everybody out for the holiday, so the only kids who remained were the ones who were critical. There was a baby who had been in a car accident, a little girl named Jennifer who had a brain tumor, a little girl named Julie with Reye's syndrome, a boy with cystic fibrosis, and Ryan. They could all die. I saw such pain in those other parents. All of us were going through the same agony. We held hands and waited and hardly spoke.

The boy with cystic fibrosis was on the other side of the curtain from Ryan. They never opened that curtain. You could hear them whispering over there; you could hear the horrible sound of them suctioning him out. Then all of a sudden he wasn't in his room anymore. His bed was empty. I knew he had died.

We were sleeping in the waiting room. Wayne visited. So did Steve. Tommy and his wife, Deb, and Mom and Dad were always there. The Reverend Harold Williams from our church came a couple of times every week.

I wanted to scream. But I couldn't. I wanted my family to think I was in control. Andrea understood that I was at my wit's end. She was the sweetest thing, trying to be this real grown-up girl. "Mom, can I go get you something to drink?" she would say. "Mom, do you want a candy bar?" They would let her go into intensive care only once a day for ten minutes to see Ryan. Sometimes I'd try to sneak her in. She sat on my lap and hugged me and held my hand.

We kept a picture of Jesus on Ryan's wall. Nancy Trent and her husband, Bob, who attended our church, brought him a little guardian angel, a plastic statue of a small girl with golden hair. It ran on batteries. Each night we'd pray together: "Thank you, Lord, for another day." When I left, I'd make sure that his guardian angel was lit. It got to mean so much, that little statue. Ryan became real agitated one time when he woke up in the middle of the night, and found that a nurse had shut it off.

"Never do that!" he yelled. "My mom does that! She shuts it off when she comes in. That way I know when she's here."

Finally, the day before Christmas, Meredith, the social worker at Riley Hospital, helped us secure a room at Ronald McDonald House. I knew we had to go there, because everybody needed a decent bed, a decent meal . . . but once I got Andrea set, I couldn't stand being away from Ryan and I went back to the waiting room. I felt helpless. The waiting time seemed endless. I kept thinking: *This is not happening.* I thought I was going crazy. I was eating myself up, trying to figure out how to tell Ryan about his disease. I was waiting for the exact right time, when his tubes would be out and he'd be feeling better. I so didn't want this announcement to be made against a background of hopelessness and despair. However, one of the doctors warned me to tell Ryan soon . . . because the news would soon start leaking out. Hospital staff would go home and tell their families. Other young patients would tell their friends. Rumors would begin to spread.

Up to that time, there had been no publicized cases of children with AIDS. This was one of the very first. The doctors and nurses kept calling Ryan's case "extraordinary" because it was the first to prove that the disease could be caught from the factor. They knew he wasn't gay, they knew he wasn't an IV drug user, they knew he had never received a transfusion. Factor VIII was the only possible cause. They kept warning me that this case was bound to attract media attention. They wanted me to tell Ryan as soon as possible because it would be terrible if he heard it from somebody else or, even worse, from the TV news.

When I saw him on Christmas Eve morning, he looked a thousand times better. The tubes were out. He still had the heart monitor, but the pads were off his eyes and he smiled at me. I thought, *Maybe now I'll tell him.* Then I thought, *No. After Christmas. When he's received his new computer, and he's looking forward to going home and playing those new computer games . . .*

The next day, on Christmas morning, I went over to the I.U. Med Center to get breakfast—and suddenly heard myself being paged. It was my mother. She was terribly upset.

"I don't know how to tell you this, Jeanne, but you've been robbed. We went over to your house to get the Christmas presents and it felt cold in there, and it turned out somebody had broken the window in the back door and let themselves in and stolen them all. We can see the footprints in the snow. We know where they were headed. The police are here . . . but they say they can't do anything . . ."

They had taken the computer I had bought for Ryan; the VCR I'd bought for Andrea so she could study her skating tapes. (They took the tapes, too. My precious memories of my little girl's earliest skating meets, all gone.) In the midst of this terrible crisis, my kids' Christmas had been stolen.

My parents filed a report—but the police said they could not get a search warrant on Christmas Day. Anyway, I couldn't think about it now.

The family of the little girl with Reye's syndrome, Julie, must have heard about the robbery. The aunt and the grandma went out and found an open drugstore and bought my kids a whole bunch of presents: a Care Bear and paint sets, a train, coloring books, crayons, whatever they could find. Sometimes strangers are so sweet and good and kind, it just fills up your heart. I will never forget those wonderful people. I still have the Care Bear and the train, and I set them under the tree at Christmas.

On Christmas Day, Wayne arrived with presents. When he heard that I hadn't yet told Ryan about his disease, he got all in a state and said, "I'm going in there and tell him right now!"

"Don't you dare!" I cried. "Let me handle this!"

Dr. Kleiman backed me up. Wayne backed off.

On the day after Christmas, Ryan felt better than he had in weeks. Reverend Williams arrived. Andrea was there in the room with us. And I told him.

"Ryan, you know you've been really sick."

Ryan said, "Yes."

"They say you have AIDS."

I saw no panic on his face.

"Does Laura know?" he asked.

"Laura, your nurse? She knows."

I guess that meant a lot to him, realizing that Laura would take care of him even though he had such a dread disease.

"Let's just pretend I don't have it," he said.

"Well, Ryan, we can't really do that. Because we have to take precautions to keep you from getting sick again."

"That's not what he means, Mom," Andrea said.

Ryan explained: "I just don't want that every time somebody enters the room, they're thinking like: Oh, poor Ryan, he's dying."

Here I was, trying to be supportive and explaining things to him, and he understood everything and was explaining them to me.

When somebody tells you that somebody you love is going to die, the first thing you think is: There's no way I can live without that person because I love that person so much. When they told me about Ryan, I really understood how awful it must be for people who've been married for fifty or sixty years to lose each other, to be so accustomed to someone and then have them taken away. Of course you wouldn't want to live.

But the truth is, you have to go on.

It's just too easy to say, "I can't do it."

It finally dawned on me how precious life was when I realized that Ryan's was going to be shortened.

They told me he had three to six months to live. I thought: I have to do everything for him in the time he has left, every single thing I can. But in my heart I believed I was going to get a miracle. As the months went by and then the years went by, I thought the miracle would surely come. Nobody had more people praying over them than Ryan did.

Later, when his life ended, I asked: "God, why? Why didn't I get a miracle? Wouldn't it have been great to show the world that You healed this boy? So everybody could see Your miraculous power?"

Now I have the feeling that when I get to Heaven, God's going to say: "You know what? You had a miracle. Ryan was only supposed to live three to six months, and he lived five and half years, and look, you're still not happy."

Chapter 3

The Strength to Never Ask Why

I was mad at everybody, but I didn't know who to blame.

I couldn't understand why Ryan had been chosen. How could my son be one of the first children, one of the first hemophiliacs, to come down with this disease? They had given us this drug that we thought was going to be such a miracle drug and help hemophiliacs live normal lives. And now they were telling us it was the drug that had given him the disease that was going to kill him. He couldn't live with it and he couldn't live without it. Now, how fair was that?

I kept asking, "Why Ryan? Why our family. WHY? WHY?"

But Ryan never asked, "Why me?"

In the hospital, he had had a vision.

"I've got to talk to you a minute, Mom."

"What is it, hon?"

"Last night, the Lord came and spoke to me."

"What? Well, what did He say?"

"He told me I had nothing to fear, that I was going to be taken care of."

"Now, Ryan, are you sure it wasn't a doctor or a nurse dressed in a white gown?"

"No, Mom."

"Well, what did He look like?"

"He sure didn't look like that picture of Jesus on my wall. From now on," he continued, "every night I'm going to thank the Lord for another day."

"All right, hon, that's exactly what we'll do."

And so we did. Every night we sat together before we went to sleep and thanked God for another day.

I had heard many stories about people talking to the Lord, and I don't know whether I ever believed them. But when Ryan told me about his vision, I believed. I saw this inner peace in him after that. What makes somebody understand what is happening to them and accept it and be able to deal with it the way Ryan did? How is it possible for a young child to release that bitterness and that anger, especially when he had a mother who was just overwhelmed by the unfairness of it all? For Ryan to have the inner strength never to ask "why," well, I think only God gives that to you.

After Christmas, little by little, he began to get better. It's almost impossible to explain the joy I felt at every little event as it happened—every tube that came out of his body, every spoonful of lime

Jell-O he kept down, the way his eyes brightened and his smile returned day by day, these little moments felt like huge victories. When he was first diagnosed, Ryan had gotten down to fifty-seven pounds. Now when he gained an ounce, even part of an ounce, I was so wild with happiness, I wanted to cheer. I had thought that I might not ever see him breathing on his own again . . . and here it was, January 24, 1985, and he was leaving the hospital, inhaling the cold winter wind and laughing.

By the time Ryan came home, I was going broke. Not two months of catastrophic illness, and a hard-working American family with good jobs and health insurance rolled to the very brink of financial ruin. From what I heard by talking to other folks in the waiting rooms of hospitals, what happened to me happens to just about everybody.

Never in my life had I expected to receive a nickel of charity from any source. But I was trapped between my need to care for Ryan and my pride, and my pride had to be sacrificed. I was thrilled to hear from Meredith, the Riley Hospital social worker, about a special fund which made up for the missed paycheck of parents who needed to stay off work to be with their children. Apparently somebody who was a millionaire who lost his daughter to cancer had made this money available. Like Ronald MacDonald house, it was a real life saver. I received a check to replace my normal take-home pay every week for six weeks.

My friends at Delco had taken up a collection for us after the robbery, to help me pay the bills that weren't medical bills covered by insurance, like house payments and car payments and gas and food. And luckily, Wayne never missed one child-support payment.

Deep down, underneath all his drunken anger and confusion, I believe there lives a devoted father.

The news that Ryan had AIDS quickly spread through Kokomo. The schoolteachers who had visited Ryan reported back. My co-workers and relatives at the plant already knew, and everyone told everybody else. Andrea told her friends without hesitation. At our church, Reverend Williams led the congregation in prayers for Ryan. There was a little article in the newspaper that didn't give Ryan's name but just noted that a Howard County child had come down with AIDS. Everyone we spoke to expressed deep concern. We were shown a lot of sympathy, and nobody seemed afraid.

Ryan weighed less than sixty pounds when he came home. My whole life began to revolve around taking care of him and getting him well again and putting some meat on him. Dr. Kleiman insisted that I do anything in my power to get Ryan to eat. He didn't care if Ryan ate fast food and Twinkies, as long as he ate. Most of the time, food just flushed right through him and gave him no nourishment. But he did seem to be able to keep down little bits of food better than whole meals. So I cooked all the time, and fed Ryan all the time, anything he wanted. If he craved something special—Denny's beef stew, hot chocolate from the Waffle House—I'd take him out anywhere, any time of the day or night, to get it.

Mom made him the meat loaf and chicken-with-noodles that he had always loved. However, the fact that he had taken so many medications had just about destroyed his ability to enjoy the mild flavors of regular old Indiana cooking. (Nobody ever tells you about this little side effect of taking medicine. Your medication may be covered by insurance, but then it creates a taste disorder in the patient that can run up some big food bills—and they are *not* covered by insurance.)

The first negative reaction we got was when one restaurant owner destroyed our dishes and our silverware. Ryan was upset, but I told him the man was probably just an ignorant person who didn't understand that AIDS could not be transmitted by sharing utensils. I was too happy to be upset. Because Ryan was miraculously gaining weight, ounce by ounce, and feeling a lot better. *Maybe they're wrong,* I dared to think. *Maybe Ryan is going to beat this thing.*

Folks in the hospital had told me that AmFAR (the American Foundation for Aids Research) had the best, latest information about AIDS. I hesitated calling them at first, because I knew many people at AmFAR were gay men. But I wanted Ryan to live. I needed to know everything, to hear from the caretakers who had seen dozens of AIDS patients, to pick their brains, absorb their knowledge and understanding. Whether or not it suited my prejudice, that meant talking to the gay community.

Terry Beirn at AmFAR had already heard about Ryan's case. He and Mike Callan and Sally Morrison were so kind and receptive to me, and so helpful. It became very easy to trust them because they were going through the same thing I was. Once you have AIDS, you're just like everybody else who has AIDS; you're all fighting to stay alive. Terry and Mike told me about new drugs, warned me about side effects, comforted me when I felt desperate. I trusted them completely. They became my closest friends and allies in the battle to save Ryan's life.

As the winter ended, Ryan began calling me at work, asking me to arrange for him to visit school. I kept putting off the call. I thought: *He's doing so well. Do I really want him around all those germs from the other kids at school?* But Ryan kept bugging me.

So finally I called and spoke to the principal, Mr. Colby, and told him Ryan was feeling better and wanted to come visit and see some of his friends. Mr. Colby was real nice and said to call him back after spring break.

We took a vacation and went down to see my sister and her family in Alabama. It was just great the way Janet and Leo took us all in and made us all comfortable. We sorely needed some time in the sun, and couldn't have afforded any other kind of vacation.

During that vacation, Ryan swung on a rope across the river; he rode his bike again; you could feel the happiness bubbling up inside him as his health returned. He played with my sister's three kids in Birmingham, went to a zoo and seemed to have contracted nothing, so I felt much easier in my mind about having him visit school. When we arrived home, I called the school again.

"Can we arrange this visit now, Mr. Colby?"

"Have you talked to the Board of Health, Mrs. White?"

"No."

"You need to talk to them. They're considering putting a quarantine sign on your front door. The school system has to abide by their rules . . ."

I could hear that he was having a real hard time talking to me. Folks sounded no less nervous at the local Board of Health. They had already dropped the quarantine idea, but they were waiting for guidelines from the State Board of Health. They were afraid of a lawsuit if they let Ryan go to school, and afraid of a lawsuit if they didn't.

I still didn't get it. I believed what I was told. Ryan was eager to return to class and decided he would take summer school. He was worried that he was going to have to take the seventh grade over again. He didn't want people to think he was dumb, and also, he didn't want the rest of his friends to be moving on up to the high school and leaving him behind.

He expected to live. There was no way to stop him from enjoying that expectation. *In fact, it was the only thing he had that was really contagious.*

Late in July 1985, a skating friend of Andrea's named Sarah Buck came to visit with us for a few days so the girls could practice together. I went to work as usual. Sometime during the morning, I received a phone call. It was Channel 8 TV. They asked me whether I'd heard that the school board had decided not to readmit Ryan.

I was so shocked, I just broke down and wept. My friend Ava shook her head.

"You didn't really think they were going to let Ryan back into school, did you?" she asked.

"Yes, I did. I thought, with the state guidelines coming and with all the official doctors saying it was fine and more people being educated about AIDS and everything, they'd say okay. Why not? WHY NOT?!"

She looked at me with such pity, as though I were just about the world's biggest fool. My naïveté, and my total absorption in getting Ryan well, kept me from realizing the truth—which was that from day one, from the time those teachers visited Riley and reacted with terror, Western School District was determined not to let Ryan return.

As soon as I got home from work, I told Ryan. He was very upset. The phone was ringing off the hook. The local news. The national news. "What are you going to do, Mrs. White? Are you going to sue? Are you going to court?" *Good Morning America.* The *Today* show. *CBS Morning News.*

"I don't know what I'm going to do."

"Can you come to New York and be on our show tomorrow morning?"

"No! How can I do that?! I have a job! I have children! There's a little girl who's staying with us who's a skating partner of Andrea's . . ."

The minute I said that, it dawned on me: *Sarah's parents have no qualms about sending her to stay with us. Because they know they have nothing to fear. Why can't Western School Board be as smart as Sarah's parents? This whole thing is just a matter of educating people and calming their fears!*

Filled with enthusiasm to help the world learn that AIDS couldn't be spread by casual contact, I got Sarah's parents' permission and packed up all three kids and flew to New York.

That was the beginning of a media siege. I know that it wasn't really Ryan they were interested in at first. The school board had made its decision against the background of the stunning revelation that Rock Hudson had AIDS. The whole dumbfounded country was immediately engaged in this issue. How many more famous people were secretly gay and hiding their illness? Ryan was trying to hide nothing. So he was a natural for television interviews, newspaper and magazine articles. The media seemed to understand something that nobody in Kokomo had figured out, including me—that this was an important story because it represented the tip of a deadly iceberg. We were having a plague. Not just *them*, but *us*.

Everybody wanted to know what I was going to do, and I had no idea. Ryan was feeling well. He kept saying he wanted to go to school. The idea of having him sitting home, spending the last years of his life watching reruns, made us all sick at heart. I inquired at the local Christian school. They said they were full—and anyway, they were much too expensive. Public school was going to be our only alternative.

Two important people strongly supported Ryan's desire to go to school. The first was Dr. Woodrow A. Myers Jr., the State Health Commissioner. He was a big, tall, African-American man, a native son of Indiana, who had been educated at Stanford and Harvard and, despite prejudice, had risen to the top ranks of the white medical establishment. He had been working in San Francisco during the first terrible outbreak of AIDS. He had seen what havoc and hysteria could be caused when health authorities and the public were unprepared for a new disease. He didn't want that to happen in Indiana. He authorized a statewide information campaign to assure the public that nobody could give anybody AIDS by breathing the same air or touching the same doorknob or using the same toilet. Citizens were told over and over that you couldn't get AIDS from saliva or sweat or kissing or tears. You could get it only from having unprotected sex with an infected person or from direct blood contact with infected blood.

The other important person who supported Ryan's desire to go to school was a lawyer, Charles Vaughan. We had met Mr. Vaughan during an unsuccessful suit against the blood companies by six hemophilia families whose loved ones had contracted AIDS from infected Factor. The suit was thrown out because in Indiana you can't sue the blood suppliers. With the start of the media blitz, the confident, feisty Mr. Vaughan began to tell me that, by legal means, we could win the right for Ryan to go back to school. He was prepared to represent us on a pro bono basis.

I thought: *There's no way we can win. We're losers from the start. Because even if we win and they let Ryan go back, he could die before he ever gets to attend classes.*

Ryan didn't see it that way. He wanted to sue. He was as determined as I was indecisive. Somebody made a joke about him at school—"What do faggots eat? Ryan White bread"—and his friend Chris was suspended for three days for hitting the kid who said it. Ryan hated that—having other people fight his battles. He wanted to fight himself.

"Come on, Mom, let's take them to court."

"I've got to weigh this thing out, hon."

"I want to go to school."

"They'll make fun of you. They'll say awful things to you. Can you handle that?"

He regarded me with patience and heaved a sigh. Had I forgotten that he was the one already handling hemophilia and AIDS?

"I can handle anything, Mom."

Mr. Vaughan grinned at me across his big desk and said with confidence, "I guess Ryan is my client now, Mrs. White."

The story of our legal battle is a matter of record now. It lasted for about a year, but it felt like a century. It aged me; it exhausted me; it strengthened me. When it was over, I was not the same person I had been when it began.

On July 30, 1985, Western School Corporation denied Ryan the right to return to school.

On August 3, the Indiana State Board of Health issued guidelines for admitting AIDS patients to school. Under these guidelines, Ryan could legally have been admitted.

On August 8, we sued in federal court to get him admitted to school.

On August 12, parents of Kokomo school children signed 117 claim forms threatening a civil suit if Ryan were allowed in.

On August 15, about fifty teachers voted to support the decision to keep Ryan out.

The next day, a federal judge ruled that we had to exhaust administrative appeals (for example, to the Department of Education) before the case could be heard in federal court.

When classes began on August 26, Ryan was linked to them from home by a computer telephone hookup.

On November 25, the Indiana Department of Education hearing officer ruled that Ryan must be admitted to school.

On December 17, the Western School Board voted unanimously to appeal the ruling.

On February 6, 1986, the appeal was answered. The Indiana Department of Education Appeals Board ruled that there was nothing to prevent Ryan from attending class if he was cleared by the Howard County Health Officer.

On February 13, the Health Officer certified that Ryan was fit to attend class.

On February 21, Ryan returned to school. Out of 360 students, 151 stayed home and seven transferred to other schools. That very same day, a Concerned Citizens group received a restraining order from Judge Brubaker that kept Ryan out of school. So no sooner did he get back in than he was out again.

On April 9, Ryan's case was argued before the higher court.

On April 10, the restraining order was dissolved. Ryan went back to school immediately. Twenty-seven kids went home rather than stay in the same building with him.

On April 22, a home school opened in Russiaville, Indiana, for students whose parents didn't want them to attend with Ryan.

Meanwhile, some parents appealed the court's ruling. On April 30, a judge vacated their arguments and upheld the earlier decision.

On July 18, the Indiana Court of Appeals dismissed the appeal of parents who did not want Ryan allowed to attend school.

On August 21, the Howard County Health Department examined Ryan and declared him fit to go to his classes.

On August 25, 1986, he began eighth grade at Western Middle School.

Every minute of the short time that he was there was hell.

The smut, the spite and the malice that surrounded us were beyond belief. They wrote filthy words on his locker. They accused him of spitting on vegetables in the supermarket. They said that, when angered, he would bite people; that he urinated on the walls in public places. They said I was a front for the gay community, a slut who slept with bisexual men and brought the disease home to my son. I still remember the hate mail, the letters that called me a whore, the pictures of me clipped from the press, on which somebody had drawn a penis in my mouth. At work, they wouldn't drink from the same water fountain as I. Some son of a gun was always sticking "Get out!" notes on my time card. I'd rip them off. He'd put them on again. Articles were posted calling Ryan a danger to the community, and asking why we didn't just do the decent thing and go off to a desert island and disappear. The evangelist Jerry Falwell suggested just that—a leper-colony-type exile, where AIDS patients could be shipped to and kept in isolation.

We got dozens of letters from the religious right, telling us that AIDS was God's punishment on my son. Frankly, up to that time, I thought *I* was a member of the religious right. So I dismissed these letter writers as nutcases and didn't pay them any mind and couldn't imagine any important person would agree with them until I met Senator Jesse Helms of North Carolina.

People I had known forever just stopped speaking to me. Generally, the women were much worse than the men. Some of my old friends didn't want their kids hanging around with my kids. My supervisor, Mike Hedrick, and the guys at work seemed to take it better.

People who supported me were attacked. Chris MacNeil of *The Kokomo Tribune* covered our story when other reporters refused to enter our home. He got death threats. Finally he moved away and found a different job. Marcia Blacklidge, recognized as a friend of our family, was ostracized by women at her gym who didn't want to sit in the hot tub with her.

The minister asked what I needed. I told him, "Gas for the trips back and forth to the hospital, and food."

The folks at our church wanted to do the right, charitable Christian thing and help out a family in trouble—but lots of them were on the side of the school board and the Concerned Citizens group, and they wanted to make sure we didn't use their money for legal fees. *So they gave me gift certificates!* For the gas station! For Kroger's Market!

And then, when I'd go shopping, some people would stare bold as you please into my shopping cart to see if I was buying something they thought was too extravagant, or something that wasn't for Ryan, like beer or wine or cigarettes.

When Ryan finally did get back to school in August 1986, his treatment there was nightmarish. Somebody broke into his locker and scrawled homophobic obscenities all over his school folders. *Faggot!* they said. *Get butt-fucked!* Nobody wanted to sit next to him in class. When he walked down the hall, the kids would flatten themselves against the walls and yell, "There he goes! The AIDS kid! Stay back!" Or they'd run up and touch him, then touch other kids and say, "Now you've got it."

I began to feel completely paranoid about my fellow citizens. I didn't know whom to trust—so I trusted no one.

My poor mother seemed to suffer worse than anybody. She took every insult right to heart. She brooded and tried to answer back. But you can't answer people who are already walking away from you.

Mom was so frustrated, so helpless to help me. All she wanted to do was to share my pain . . . but in her effort to share the pain, she only compounded it. The more I knew of her anguish, the guiltier I felt for being powerless to protect her.

The result was that I began to dread her phone calls. When she would begin telling me what her sisters had heard at the plant, what so-and-so said to her and what she said back, I reacted with something close to hostility. I didn't want to hear all the bad talk. I felt like if I didn't hear it, then I could imagine for a few moments that it wasn't happening, and take a rest from my own paranoia and isolation.

In the churches of Kokomo, they prayed for Ryan. That was the way everybody prefaced their testaments of sympathy—and their rejection. "We pray for Ryan; he is in our prayers. But . . ." It was a big "but." At our church, our family was asked to sit in the middle of a pew in the back. One Christmas, I was thrilled to hear some of our parishioners singing carols outside our door. I invited them in for hot chocolate. They were afraid to enter the house. One Easter, when we were all supposed to join hands and pray, a man whom my father had known since boyhood refused to take Ryan's hand.

My father was devastated. And Ryan was deeply affected as well.

I told my kids: "You cannot worry about what other people

think of you. You must do what is necessary and right, and go on with your life."

One day when Ryan was being released from the hospital, the Reverend Bud Probasco, who had been visiting with him, walked out with us. We said our good-byes and then Ryan turned to me and said, "Mom, I want Bud Probasco to do my funeral." The reverend had been the assistant minister at our church, then moved on to another pulpit. He visited Ryan several times. They had a good relationship. But I was shocked when Ryan brought it up. It stunned me that he was planning his own funeral. Then I thought: *Well, so be it. It's Ryan's life and he should be able to chose the preacher he wants praying over him if at any time his life does end.*

Then somebody shot at our house. We found the bullet hole in our big picture window. My brave girl, Andrea, was simply too terrified to sleep. I felt sick with confusion. I prayed for a way we could somehow leave this mess. I prayed for acceptance. I kept telling myself: *Just do your thing, Jeanne. As long as you believe you're right, as long as you have not done anything wrong, you're okay. You are not a bad mother. You are not a bad person. Ten years down the road, these folks are going to be sorry.*

Dr. Martin Kleiman was a fairly conservative physician, I think. He did not jump at the news of every exciting possible drug as we did. When Ryan was in Riley Hospital with a stomach infection, he tried five or six different antibiotics until he found one that worked. In his quiet, gentle way, he could be very persistent. He acquired AZT for Ryan even though Ryan wasn't yet sixteen, the required age for a prescription. One day I called AmFAR, and Mike Callan asked me how much AZT Ryan was getting. When I told him, he was shocked. "Cut that dosage in half!" he insisted. "Too much can cause liver damage."

I was so afraid of offending Dr. Kleiman that I just cut the dosage in half without telling him. Six months later, he told me, "We have to cut down Ryan's dosage of AZT because there are reports of side effects." When I admitted that I had already done that, he smiled and wasn't mad at all. He knew that in those early days of AIDS, there was what he called "a very useful grapevine" which brought information to patients long before it reached practitioners.

His protocol was to make my boy feel as well as he could possibly feel, to treat his symptoms in a way that would keep him out of the hospital as much as possible. This meant keeping him off intravenous, not rushing to put him on a feeding tube. One time there was a gathering of AIDS patients down by NIH in Washington. Ryan didn't want to go there and have to stay in a hospital for three or four days. Every day that he wasn't in the hospital, he felt like, "Yes!! I lived this day! I was not sick this day." Dr. Kleiman concluded that nothing the doctors could have done for him would have helped Ryan as much as one more day of living like a well boy. He let him out of the NIH appearance.

I was very lucky to have found a doctor who never hesitated to say what he didn't know, who protected us against the "nutty" cures but never made us feel foolish because we placed our hopes in them, and who understood that no amount of science could quite explain the healing power of the human mind. He let Ryan do things that Ryan was clearly too sick to do . . . because he knew he would be less sick if he did them.

He gave Ryan his home number. He promised him solemnly that he would never prescribe any treatment that he would not prescribe for his own children. He never talked down to me. If I wanted something, or if Ryan wanted something, he moved heaven and earth to make it happen. It got so that Ryan wouldn't have anything done if he wasn't absolutely sure that Dr. Kleiman wanted it done.

Ryan learned a lot about doctoring from being Dr. Kleiman's patient and reading *Time* magazine. I'll never forget one incident that occurred about a year after Ryan was diagnosed. Mom and Dad had come to stay with him while I was at work. Dad had gone out for lunch with my brother. When Dad returned, he looked kind of pale. He was sweating on a cold day.

"I feel kind of funny," Dad said, "Think I'll go lie down."

"Grandpa, listen," Ryan said. "You can't lie down. You have to go right to the hospital. You're having a heart attack."

Dad went to the hospital and ended up with a quadruple bypass.

Dr. Kleiman and Ryan talked in the privacy of the hospital, in those deep night hours when the day is turned upside down and they were awake and everybody else was sleeping. I suppose their relationship stood in somewhat for the father-son relationship that Ryan missed so sorely. Even if he had never had AIDS, Ryan would have been a very smart boy, a dedicated student. He needed somebody who represented the well-educated world to talk to him, to be his friend. Dr. Kleiman was the man on the spot.

Nothing shocked me so greatly as the hostility of the other victims of hemophilia in our community. I had expected them to be supportive. Instead, they treated me like Typhoid Mary.

We had twelve hemophiliacs in Howard County. As soon as I understood how the Factor was made, how the blood was bought from anyone who would give it, I knew that all the Factor must be infected and all the hemophiliacs in terrible danger.

I kept saying to the people I knew who were hemophiliacs or were living with hemophiliacs: "Don't you see? The gay community is already being blamed for causing this disease. Soon the hemophiliacs will be blamed as well. They're going to start unknowingly giving it to their wives and their children. This has to be discussed now!"

But it was too painful to face the fact of AIDS; it was too complicated to explain to an ignorant, jittery public what hemophilia was exactly, that "hemo" wasn't "homo." The lawyer for the Hemophilia Association spent more than an hour on the phone with me, trying to convince me that the members could not afford to be associated with AIDS. "This is a hemophilia organization," he said, "not an AIDS organization."

I couldn't believe it. There was a hemophilia clinic at the mall where they were passing out brochures and information, and they didn't want me to come anywhere near it.

In 1985, when the clinics brought in all the hemophiliacs and started testing them, they found that more than 80 percent of them had AIDS.

Every day throughout the conflict between Ryan and the school board and then the Concerned Citizens group, I thought of giving up. Every single day I considered it. I was so close sometimes, my hand was on the phone, ready to call Mr. Vaughan and tell him I was throwing in the towel. My brother and sister wanted me to. They were afraid for our poor mother, who was close to a nervous breakdown.

I was at the end of my strength, and ready to listen to those who told me to withdraw. I was not prepared to sacrifice Ryan and Andrea and Mom and everything in my life in order to continue with a crusade just because I believed it was right. *All right*, I thought. *That's it. You've got to give up.*

And I would have, too—except for something that happened in the winter of 1986.

In February, a physician had certified that Ryan was fit to attend class and a Howard County judge refused a request by parents to issue an injunction to keep him home. On February 21, 1986, he returned to school, but 151 out of 360 students stayed home. Because the school district didn't have enough money to go on fighting, the parents had organized their own legal action. They hired a lawyer and had a meeting. I recall that it was on a Wednesday night, and a friend of mine who was there reported to me about it.

What the Concerned Citizens of Kokomo planned to do was have me declared an unfit mother, have Ryan taken away from me and placed in foster care, then have his foster parents keep him out of school until he died. All the reasoning behind this scheme had been worked out. I would be declared "unfit" because I was trying to send a child with AIDS to school, thereby exposing him to all kinds of bacteria which he would not be able to fight off because of his disease and which would ultimately kill him. It wouldn't be a problem to get this ruling from the child welfare authorities because some of them, too, were "Concerned Citizens" and would support whatever the parents' group wanted to do. No less than three families were already lined up as prospective foster parents for Ryan. (What these folks were going to do with Andrea I do not know, but I'm sure they would have figured out something.) According to the reports that came to me, some folks advised that this plan seemed horribly cruel and just the attempt would create adverse publicity for their cause. They dropped the idea.

Proof of how powerful and well connected these people were in the town was demonstrated on February 21, the day that Ryan went back to school. That very afternoon, with phenomenal speed, a local judge issued a restraining order to keep Ryan out of school. The crowd burst into wild cheers of joy. They jumped and embraced and whooped and hollered as though the Hoosiers had just won the national championship.

The story of the parents' meeting and the delirious joy in the courtroom when Ryan was defeated did something to me. I felt like I had entered a new psychological state. I wasn't fighting for his education anymore; I wasn't even fighting for my boy's right to go to school. I was fighting hatred, plain and simple. Some sort of lead thing got into my gut. I set my teeth together in my jaw and straightened my back.

I realized that Ryan, my strong son, was absolutely right when he said, "We're going to educate these people one way or another, Mom, or die trying."

People always ask me: Where did you find your strength to go on? My answer is that I grew into my strength. It came to me when I thought things through and found my purpose. All of a sudden, you ask yourself: "Now what is the object in all this? It's for Ryan to get back to school. Let's get him back to school and get it over with and end this period of chaos in our lives." I started learning that no matter what comes back at you, you've got to say what you feel and mean what you say.

You're sick and tired of it; you're sick of the dispute just lingering on and people just drawing it out, making it last, hoping he's going to die; and all of a sudden, one day you just get fed up. You say: "I'm going to do the right thing, even if it isn't the easy thing." And that's all there is to that.

Chapter 4

Guardian Angels

I t took a long time before I felt like I was on solid ground with the media people. They intimidated me; their casual exaggerations threw me off. If I found a reporter I trusted—and I found a few, thank Heaven—I stuck with that person. But one thing I knew going in and I never veered from it and it stood me in good stead. "Tell the truth," I said to Ryan. "Never lie. Never. If you tell one lie, it has to lead to another, and then another, and then you're lost. Always tell the absolute truth and then you will not have to worry about remembering the lies you have told. If you tell the truth, people will recognize it. They will trust you."

He took that advice. He never changed his story. He never changed

himself. He was the same boy, on camera and off camera. And that is a
rare thing indeed in this two-faced world.

The media arrive on your doorstep. They ring your phone off
the hook. They demand; they plead; they're pitiful; they're imperial.
Sometimes they threaten you. Other times they love you to death.
They are the biggest asset you can have, and the biggest pain in
the butt.

I hated dealing with the media. But at the same time, I thought
if we did a few interviews, it would educate people in Kokomo and
lessen their fear of Ryan. He knew if he wanted to go back to school,
he was going to have to make it happen, and talking to the press
and the TV was the only way.

People said I forced him to make these appearances. That is a
lie. I never made Ryan do anything. However, if he said he'd do it,
I told him he couldn't change his mind, he had to stick to his
commitment.

Ryan became the love of the nation. But back in Kokomo, I
became "The Wicked Mother." No one wanted to criticize Ryan,
so I was the person who was put on trial. "I feel sorry for the kid,"
said one typical letter. "But . . . I bet his mother loves all this
publicity. I bet she's not turning down the money she's getting from
TV and magazines. I think she should offer Kokomo an apology,
not vice versa."

I suppose I should have blown off such attacks, but to be perfectly truthful, I never could. I was still the same person who'd
cleaned up people's houses when I baby-sat for them so they would
like me. I cared what people thought. I wanted to scream from the
rooftops: "I'm not getting rich from my son's illness! If I were,

I would have escaped from this mean, ignorant town in a New York minute!"

One day I felt weak, like I was going to cry any minute; other times I felt real strong. My son kept his sense of humor. Not me. I sank into anger. When I saw myself on TV, I thought: *Boy, I look mean, I look hard. I look like an ugly person.* I think I looked that way because I didn't know who to trust, or what to say. I was scared. Scared of saying something wrong or doing something wrong. My own anger welling up inside scared me worst of all. You get so sick of trying to explain yourself and trying to make people understand, you just want to scream. Every time I got to one of those moments when I wanted to fight back so much that I was ready to get mad and yell, I would force my mouth to stay shut and pray: "Oh, Lord, please help me not to say anything I'm going to be sorry for later!"

The greatest thing about the media people was that they weren't afraid to be with Ryan. They replaced the kids who wouldn't play with him, the teachers who wouldn't educate him. Taro Yamasaki, a photographer from *People*, did a photo essay on him and gained his trust and friendship. So did Dilip Menta, an Indian photographer from *Picture Week* and *Time*, who enchanted Ryan with tales of his worldwide travels. The lively blond reporter Carrie Jackson from Channel 13 became a real close friend to our family.

These folks were sharp and smart and friendly. They were Ryan's home school; they brought the world back into his isolated, lonely life. Most important, they made him feel worthwhile because they thought he was doing something important, by going public about AIDS.

One casualty of the media blitz was my daughter. Andrea became absolutely phobic about reporters. She was a young girl, hearing all these terrible things about her mother and her brother, and the reporters were always popping in the door, peeking in the windows, sticking microphones in her face. No wonder she was turned off.

When Ryan returned to school so briefly in February 1986 (before the Concerned Citizens group got him thrown out again), there was a tremendous media crush. Some of the reporters arrived there at three or four in the morning to find a place in front. I called Steve Ford and asked him if he would take Ryan and Andrea and their friend Heath to school. He immediately accepted.

He looked strong and confident, walking with those kids to school. I kept thinking: *How do I get that way? How can I learn to stand up to people like that?*

AIDS was such a mystery back then that every idea seemed worth a try. We heard about a new one every day. Heat the blood. Exchange the blood. Give him smallpox to jump-start his immune system. Feed him this; soak him in that. Eliminate pork. Drink peroxide. The media were reporting on treatments I could not even pronounce. While I was busy investigating one, they would announce another.

Dr. Kleiman said, "These cures are wacko, Jeanne." I nodded respectfully—but half the time I went right home and started calling all over the country to find out more about them.

Our garage was filled to the ceiling with cures and potions from all over the world. We received every kind of vitamin in every denomination, cases of ginseng, garlic, mineral baths, milk shakes. People sent them out of the goodness of their hearts, motivated by a sincere desire to help. Nobody ever asked me for any money for these things.

Alternative medicine didn't daunt me in the least.

We had all these ministers calling and wanting to pray over Ryan, saying they could heal him.

At first I let them all come, even those who seemed obviously insane. I kept hearing my grandma Helen with her caution about the beggar at the door who might be Jesus or one of His angels. I was afraid to turn away someone who might be the Lord in disguise. I was determined not to overlook anything or anyone who might have the answer. I didn't care how my boy was cured: I just didn't want him to die.

The preachers would enter the house, they would pray, they would pull on Ryan's legs, stretch his back, then wait for the disease to depart from his body. Ryan's faith in all this began to deteriorate quickly.

One couple called from Russiaville, where Western Middle School is. They said they had gone out for a long walk one evening and the Lord had appeared to them and told them that the conflict between Ryan and Western School Board would evaporate if Ryan didn't have AIDS, and that they should visit us and pray for him. I thought they were just trying to get into my house so they could convince us to drop the suit. But that wasn't so. They turned out to be completely sincere. They came from a Methodist congregation that believed in speaking in tongues.

Now, I had never really believed in speaking in tongues. We certainly didn't do it at our church; in fact, I was shocked that any Methodist church would do it. Some believe it's the work of the devil and others believe it's a gift that comes through Christ. Something sweet about these people made me let them in.

We stood in a circle and held hands and they prayed. All of a sudden the man began speaking in this strange language that wasn't comprehensible, and then his wife was doing it, and then I was doing it, too. I was surprised and shocked. Although my brother, Tommy, believed in speaking in tongues, I never had—and I certainly would not have believed I could do it. I wasn't frightened when it was happening. I was calm. I was in control, but out of control at the same time. I didn't know what I was saying, but I wanted to know. It seemed to me like a real lovely prayer. I felt that the Lord was speaking through me, and I thought: *I want to know what He is saying!* Because even though it was my voice, it wasn't like me talking.

The couple declared that pretty soon the Lord would come to me and tell me what I had said, and they hugged us and left, secure that they had done all that the Lord wanted them to do to help Ryan.

This wonderful sense of exhilaration came over me. Speaking in tongues was the most beautiful experience I had ever had. It made me feel very, very special. I know it was not evil, because it was just so beautiful. Maybe I was in a trance. But I remember what happened, so I couldn't have been in a trance. I thought: *If this kind of praying has the power to transform me, then maybe it can transform my son.* I wondered after it was over if I was the only one who heard me.

"No, Mom, I heard you, too," Ryan said. "You weren't stuttering. The voice that came out of your mouth was your voice. But I couldn't understand what you were saying."

I had been a real skeptic about speaking in tongues until I did it myself. I felt very blessed by the experience. I felt the Lord was giving me a sign that He approved of me, and approved of the way I was handling this situation. I believe now that the meaning of this whole terrible trial of Ryan's illness may have been revealed to me that day when I spoke in tongues, but I have not yet found the wisdom to understand it. Maybe the Lord is not ready yet for me to hear. Or maybe the true meaning of what I said has already been revealed to me, and I just have not learned enough to understand it.

After three or four months of all these visitations, Ryan looked at me with those weary eyes of his and said, "Enough, Mom. Enough. I'm getting so fed up with all this. Please, please, no more. If the Lord's going to heal me, He's going to heal me."

"I am so sorry, hon. I just didn't want to give up hope."

"I know, Mom."

What would I have done without that boy's tenderness and understanding? Ryan was more worried about me than about himself.

The one person who really did bring Ryan enormous spiritual comfort was my brother. Tommy Joe was raised Methodist like me and Janet. We all had faith and believed. But Tommy was more open about it. He read the Bible all the time, prayed all the time and watched all the religious shows on TV. Eventually Tommy went to Pentecostal churches and Brethren churches because he didn't believe our church had enough religion. He worked at Kroger's at night, and watched the four children while his wife, who was a nurse, worked during the day. He was a great family man, did everything with his children, lived a religious life exactly the way the Lord wants.

The rest of us sometimes thought Tommy was overreligious. Then when Ryan became ill, his faith really sustained us. He and Ryan became very close. They'd sit and talk about the Lord and His teachings. Every time he visited, he would put oil on Ryan's head and say a prayer over him from James, Chapter 5.

Is anyone among you suffering? Let him pray. Is any cheerful?
Let him sing praise. Is any among you sick? Let him call for the

elders of the church and let them pray over him, anointing him with oil in the name of the Lord, and the prayer of faith will save the sick man, and the Lord will raise him up; and if he has committed sins, he will be forgiven. Therefore confess your sins to one another, and pray for one another, that you may be healed. The prayer of a righteous man has great power in its effects.

Tommy told Ryan to say that prayer every time he got scared.

It is incredible how a serious medical situation changes a family. You can't just roll out of bed and live your life anymore. Every step, every purchase, every remark has to be seen through a new light. To get over the guilt that you are well and your loved one is suffering becomes a full-time job and a gigantic emotional burden. To be able to get through it, you need advice. However, to my amazement, thousands of young people were now seeking advice from my Ryan, or wanting some kind of strength from Ryan because of their own problems. Compared to his problems, their problems suddenly didn't seem so serious; just by being himself, he was a comfort to other kids.

During the time when I was trying to get Ryan into school in Kokomo and survive the hostility of the townspeople there, I figured I had very few friends. The loneliness of my situation just made me miserable. But then, because of Ryan's exposure to the media, something happened. Perfect strangers took our cause to heart and became a new community in spirit for us to depend on.

People began to send us things. We'd receive "Get Well" cards and balloons and happy faces and flowers. A lot of the mail came from men with AIDS, and from their families. Parents wanted advice; they wanted to commiserate, to pool their strength with mine, just to talk. Young people wrote constantly to Ryan. Often they were the children of divorce who had heard that Ryan's dad and I had split. They wanted to talk to another kid who they were sure would understand. Very often, he heard from children with disabilities or their well siblings.

Sometimes folks would send us money. "Here's $20, Mrs. White. Take yourself and the kids out to dinner." Or, "Here's $25. Buy Andrea and Ryan something special." In February 1987, some kids from the Catholic Youth Organization had a talent show at Our Lady of Lourdes School in Utica, New York, called "Tryin' for Ryan," and raised $1,500, which helped us enormously. I was overwhelmed that other kids should be so incredibly generous. I couldn't get over how considerate people were, how they identified with our lives and understood what it means to be up against it.

I was always trying to figure out how I was going to have gas money or milk money, saving pennies in this big old plastic Coke bottle. Somehow people understood how we were living. They understand the phone bill, the electric bill, the mortgage payments, the bank penalty on a bounced check, the tank of gas that it takes to get you back and forth from the hospital, the regular everyday stuff that no insurance covers. I tried to write thank-you notes to every single one. But no note could adequately express my gratitude.

We had another important group of friends working on behalf of our cause, right there in Indiana. Most of these people I never met. I know now that I probably owe more to them than I can ever say.

Between January 1985, when Ryan was fighting for his life in Riley Hospital, and January 1989, Indiana's governor was Robert D. Orr, a Republican. He appointed Dr. Woodrow A. Myers Jr. as

Commissioner of Health. When the trouble between us and Western School Board began, Dr. Myers assembled a team of people who went to work to make folks in Indiana understand AIDS. Many of the people on that team were moms just like me. There was Dr. Myers's assistant Nancy Blough, an attorney. There was Kathy Lucas, a lawyer from State Attorney General Linley E. Pearson's office who became Director of Legal Affairs for the State Health Department. Dr. Judith Johnson-Deutsch, a specialist in infectious diseases, ran the campaign to educate local health and school officials. Later on, Senator Pat Miller, the Republican head of the State Senate Health and Environmental Committee, and Senator Kathy Smith, a Democrat from southeastern Indiana, pulled together with one idea in mind: to save the children of Indiana. Some folks called them "the Momteam."

At the grass-roots level, they tackled the problem of prevention. Many folks thought that everything you did to stop the spread of tuberculosis would stop the spread of AIDS. Quarantine. Isolation. Disinfection. When we were moving out of Kokomo and nobody would buy our house because it was known as "the AIDS house," a community leader called for volunteers to help her scrub the house until it was spotless, so prospective buyers would know that they could move in safely. It was the bacteria-fighting message we had all learned from Listerine and Lysol. But it had little bearing on the new viruses like HIV.

Dr. Myers and the Momteam sent nurse educators out across Indiana, explaining AIDS prevention in schools and public meetings. Unfortunately, Western Middle School turned down offers for a nurse educator to come and talk about Ryan and AIDS.

Another big problem was that the Board of Health was not in charge of school health. The school board was. The school board could bar any child with a disease spread by "normal school contact." But school board members were *elected*. They'd advertise, go on the radio, put up yard signs, just like regular politicians. So even though they might know perfectly well that "normal school contact" could not spread AIDS, they were afraid of public opinion and had to vote in such a way as to avoid political backlash.

It turned out not to be real hard to convince the local school boards to give up this "power." Few envied the Kokomo board members their job of having to judge between a sick child with a sympathetic media behind him and a terrified parent body with the political future in their hands.

Because of the incubation period—the lag time between contracting the disease and showing symptoms of it—it was just impossible to know who had AIDS. The only way to deal with the disease was to adopt "Universal Precautions," a standardized way of treating bodily fluids that would be taught to everybody from cops to athletic coaches. It was kind of like teaching everybody basic hygiene—like washing your hands after you go to the bathroom—except that this was a new, even more intimate hygiene. Control of bodily fluids to prevent AIDS meant defining what those bodily fluids were. "No, we don't mean tears, or saliva, or sweat," said Dr. Myers and his team. "We mean blood. Semen. Vaginal secretions."

That must have been some job, to get the dignified lawmakers in the Indiana State Legislature to talk about semen and vaginal secretions.

Everybody wanted to know who had AIDS. Firefighters, police, health professionals, insurance companies. If they couldn't know it person by person, they were perfectly ready to shun members of those groups showing a high incidence of HIV infection: Haitians, hemophiliacs, intravenous drug users, members of the gay commu-

nity. For every attack against these groups, there were counterdemands made by the civil liberties folks, who felt their rights had to
be protected. And then other counterdemands made by some right-
wing conservatives, who truly believed that AIDS was a vengeance
from God for immoral behavior and rightfully punishable by death.

At one point, Kathy Lucas told me, Senator Pat Miller put all
the interested parties in one room and said: "You people do not
come out of here until you iron out a solution to all these problems."

The law that was written as a result of those stormy meetings
was a real monument to the American democratic process, and it
helped Indiana face down the great plague of our time.

They called it The Ryan White Law.

I have since heard about the terrible pressures that were exerted
against Dr. Myers and the Momteam and others who supported
Ryan's right to go to school and championed a new way of looking
at AIDS in Indiana. I do not have enough words to explain how
courageous I think these people were, to stand strong and endure
on behalf of a cause they thought was just. I know there were hundreds more whose names I don't know, whose efforts I am not aware
of. But until the end of my days, I will thank them for their heroism.
How proud it makes me feel that so many citizens of my home state
just quietly fought for right and reason, and kept on fighting until
the fight was won.

*Whenever I would boil over in anger at the people who were trying
to keep Ryan out of school, it was Ryan himself who would calm me down.*

*"Mom, they're just trying to protect their own kids the way you're
trying to protect me," he'd say. "That's why we can't be angry with them.
We have to understand them and try to continue to teach them."*

So I did that, always. I tried to reverse the roles and ask myself what

I would have done if somebody else's kid had AIDS and Ryan didn't and I had to make up my mind whether to send him to school. I know I would have been scared to death. I also think I might not have been real eager to learn about AIDS if my child was not the child who had it.

But I do think I would have forced myself to calm down and listen to the experts. I don't think I would have joined the bandwagon and kept my child at home. I might have said, "Ryan, you go on to school and treat this child with sympathy and respect, but keep your distance from him . . ." But I would never have allowed him to ridicule a sick child or go on some kind of a rampage against him. Never.

My motive for continuing this horrible episode in my life was based on the belief that folks would change. I lost my anger by believing that one day these folks were going to be educated, they were going to know the truth and feel sorry for the way they had behaved. If we gave up, it would not have been any better for Ryan; our lives would not have been easier. And it wouldn't have been any better either for other AIDS sufferers in our state.

Our only hope was that folks would gradually learn about AIDS the way we had. Our hearts filled up with the certain feeling that we were right, and that meant there was no room in our hearts for anger.

My children hated Kokomo.

We had won our court case by the middle of April 1986. Ryan was back in school. (The legal appeals of the parents' group were all later thrown out by the courts.) Still, the bitterness and anger against us in our town never went away. The kids were shunned and insulted daily. "Get us out of here, Mom," they pleaded. "Please find us another place to live."

I poured out my heart to Dr. Kleiman. "How can I get my kids out of here?! Where can I go?!" He shook his head and said he didn't think it was likely I'd find any community where all the folks would accept us.

I sat at my kitchen table at night, going over bills, trying to see a way to rescue my family. I was flat broke. When Ryan would take sick and I couldn't get to work, I simply had no income. My family was giving me every dime they could spare. I never expected help from anyone, but if the mail brought a twenty-five-dollar check from some well-wisher out there in big-hearted America, I sure did appreciate it.

Andrea's skating life was all but destroyed by the lack of time and money to tend to it. She was a growing girl; she needed new skates. They were real expensive. Steve Ford had bought her the last pair. Now she had grown two sizes and she needed yet another pair. Larry, her coach, said, "Her feet are killing her, Jeanne. She can't hardly stab. She can't hardly do anything."

I got Andrea the new skates that time, by borrowing from my family and paying off the balance week by week. But she understood that it was a tremendous effort. She was missing so much skating practice because of Ryan's illness that girls she had beaten in years past were placing ahead of her at the meets. She set her mouth in a tight line, fought back the tears and said, "I'm going to quit skating, Mom. We can't afford it anymore. There's no point in going on . . ."

I couldn't even keep one young roller skater properly equipped. How was I ever going to get enough money to move out of Kokomo?

During that difficult spring, Ryan's story received a lot of media attention. He had become well known. My friend Terry Beirn at AmFAR had asked us to participate in a big fund-raising benefit for

AIDS research to be cohosted by Calvin Klein and Elizabeth Taylor, who had been great fighters in the war against AIDS. Of course I said yes to this invitation. I would do anything for AmFAR. No one had helped us more than Terry.

I eagerly anticipated going to the benefit because I thought I would meet Elizabeth Taylor. To me, she was the biggest star ever. But it turned out Ryan had other preferences. He appeared on ABC's *Good Morning America* with David Hartman, and when they asked him which celebrities he was looking forward to meeting at the benefit, he said, "Elton John. Definitely Elton John."

To be perfectly honest, I had hardly even heard of Elton John. I wasn't much of a pop-music fan. I knew he was a singer, I could recognize his name, but I couldn't match it with a face. My idea of a star was Elizabeth Taylor or Marilyn Monroe or John Wayne. A singer/songwriter who sometimes sported a pink ponytail or golden sneakers seemed like no big deal to me. Except when somebody played "Little Jeanne" on my birthday, I didn't think about Elton John or his music one way or the other.

As it turned out, Elton didn't come to the benefit. He had jet lag. Ryan was terribly disappointed. I told him, "Honey, you mustn't get caught up with these celebrities. They're not like *real* friends. They may hang around for a bit, but that's all. Don't get your hopes up, Ryan."

We arrived at the benefit at six o'clock like they told us to. We stood around for three hours. There were no tables and very few chairs, and the photographers constantly bugged Ryan to pose with this celebrity and that celebrity. *Smile! Big smile! Way to go! One more time!* I could see he was exhausted. I stood behind him so he could lean on me. Terry Beirn held on to him when he walked. We were waiting for Elizabeth Taylor. I was hoping to get her autograph and have a picture taken with her that I could show to my family back home. She finally arrived, but before I had a chance to speak to her, she was gone.

Even though I was disappointed, I still loved the AmFAR benefit. It was the first thing we had done which had nothing to do with our court battles. All Ryan's other activities, including his media appearances, concerned his struggle to go to school. This was something that was helping in the fight against AIDS itself. The experience gave him a new sense of personal security, because he realized people were proud to be around him. And now he had something to do, a cause, a sense of being part of a movement. I think that helped him live longer.

The next morning, we were on our way to the airport in a limo, me and Andrea and Ryan. And suddenly the phone rang. Who could it be? Who would know we were in this limo at this moment?

It was Elton John. I could barely understand him because of his British accent, but I finally made out that he had tracked down the limo service that was taking us to the airport and then convinced them to give him the phone number of our car. He was just calling because he had heard Ryan mention him on TV and wanted to apologize for having missed the benefit. He told Ryan he would call again to set up some good time when we could come and see him perform. *And to my astonishment, he did!* In the autumn, he called and invited the kids and me to join him for three days in Texas, where he was giving a concert.

We didn't get to go because just after school started in September, Ryan came down with a terrible cough and landed in the hospital. But just as soon as he got out, Elton John sent us three airplane tickets and brought us to California.

Elton personally toured us around Disneyland. He held a party for all the members of his band and their families, and we flew with them in his private jet to his concerts in San Diego and Oakland. When Ryan became exhausted and couldn't walk another step, Elton got hold of a wheelchair and raced him around with such energy and good nature that it didn't even seem like a wheelchair, it seemed more like a ride at an amusement park. He put us in one limo and led the way with another and sped around the warm city, stopping on the Interstate and popping out of his celebrity sunroof to wave and tell jokes. Andrea and Ryan adored him. They would have followed him anywhere.

The look on Dr. Kleiman's face when we returned and he saw Ryan's tan and his smile and examined him and found him so much better, that look of delight was the greatest tribute anybody could have paid to Elton John.

In a more serious moment during the Los Angeles trip, Elton had turned to me and asked, "What do you need, Jeanne? Not tickets to concerts, not sweatshirts and balloons; what do you need to make your life easier?"

I laughed. In the midst of all this entertainment and fun, it was almost impossible to recall my little, practical Indiana needs. What could I tell this kind man? That I needed to leave my hometown, that Kokomo needed a break from the Whites and the Whites needed a break from Kokomo? That I needed our story to die down and disappear so my parents and my kids wouldn't have to face hostility and despair every single day? My "needs" were so great that I couldn't begin to explain them. So I just said, "Oh, well, I don't need much of anything, Elton. We're okay."

I completely forgot that conversation. Then, sometime after we got home, out of the blue, Elton John sent me a check. I set it out in front of me on the kitchen table and wept all over it.

I paid my four past-due mortgage installments and brought my account up-to-date. I paid my bills. I bought a dishwasher. And a clothes dryer. And a television. And a one-year-old Chevy van. Having that van was like having a deluxe room in the wide world. Now I could begin to take Andrea to skating meets again—we could carry a cooler with our food in it, and pack all of her equipment into the van, and other skating moms and their kids could ride with us to share expenses. Now I could whiz back and forth to Riley Hospital without worrying that Ryan was hanging out impatiently waiting for me, eager to get out of there and so disappointed because the '81 diesel had been towed yet again. The sense of security, to know that when I put the key in the ignition, the engine would turn over—oh, that was so wonderful. A vanload of worry just slipped off my back.

To me and my children, Elton John was like a genie. Soon we began to feel that we really could count on him—like just what I had told Ryan celebrities could never be—a *real* friend.

Another wonderful friend we made at that time was Greg Louganis. He just called us up one day out of the blue and said he was coming to Indianapolis for the U.S. Diving championships and had decided to invite our family to watch him compete. I trembled with fear but made no protest as Greg let Ryan climb the high board. He gave Ryan the medal he won at that meet—the 38th National Title medal. After that, he developed a unique relationship with each one of us.

To Ryan, he was a tower of strength. Ryan so wanted to be an athlete like his sister; he had been very disappointed when Dr. Kleiman wouldn't give him steroids to build up his muscles. He loved being around tall, strong people like Greg and Howie Long. It was almost as though he felt their strength might leak into his body.

To Andrea, Greg was a kind of backseat coach. He encouraged her to hang in at roller-skating. He felt her time would come again, and he didn't want her to be completely out of shape when that happened. He gave her exercises, told her how to avoid leg cramps. He reinspired her. He flew to Michigan to watch her skate in the regional championships in 1990.

For me, while accompanying Ryan on his strange, sometimes dangerous trip into the world of celebrity, Greg served both as precious friend and as guide and protector. For example, he helped us understand how to react when some people decided to make Ryan's story into a television movie. Like Linda Otto of the Landsburg Company that finally bought the rights to Ryan's story, he kept warning us that just because we had sold the rights didn't mean we had sold the movie.

We received a check for $25,000 for the rights to the film. I had never seen a check for anything like that amount. For two weeks, I didn't cash it, I was too busy *looking* at it. I felt like maybe, just maybe, this money could get me and my kids out of Kokomo.

Marcia Blacklidge mentioned to a real estate agent she trusted that I might be interested in looking at homes. The lady called and said she was going to see some houses in Cicero—a little community of about four thousand people in the next county south—and invited me to come with her.

We went looking in Shorewood Estates, a lovely lakeside development. Many people in the area worked in Indianapolis, Anderson and Kokomo and commuted. The last house we looked at was a Cape Cod on Overlook Circle. It had a real country feeling. The lake. The woods. So many birds and squirrels waiting to be fed. The yard that begged for a garden. In the summer, when the leaves were on the trees, you couldn't see your neighbor. I felt as though we could regain our private lives here.

I applied for a loan with the same bank I had used for my house in Kokomo. I thought, since I had $25,000 to put down, we should be able to get a mortgage. But because I had fallen behind on my mortgage payments so often and had such a bad credit rating, the bank told me I needed to put up another $10,000. Elton John generously loaned it to me. I said I would pay him back when I got the rest of the money from the movie—or, if the movie never went forward, I would sell the house a year after Ryan died, and pay him back then.

We moved to Cicero on May 15, 1987. It was a great day.

When ABC announced that *The Ryan White Story* was a go, and Linda Otto went into production, we all went down to Statesville, North Carolina, for the movie shoot. It was great fun for Ryan and Andrea. But for me, one of the most important things about that movie was that it gave me enough money to pay back Elton John.

I didn't want to seem to be sneaking into Hamilton County, so as soon as we decided to buy the Cicero house, I called the high school and the local health department. I was scared to death. Would we face more of the same bigotry? Would we suffer the same isolation in our new home as we had in the old one? The first time somebody rang my bell, I was afraid to answer the door. It turned out to be Mary Baker and Betsy Stewart, my neighbors, welcoming me to Cicero. From then on, everything was uphill.

Our warm and friendly reception by the town of Cicero is a testament to Dr. Myers's determination to teach the people of Indiana not to fear AIDS. Deborah Taylor of the local office of the State Board of Health told the newspapers that her office had received no negative comments about our arrival. Part of the reason for that was that Jim Stewart, Betsy's husband, who was active in the Kiwanis, helped the State Board to institute a community-wide education program.

Hamilton Heights High School—its teachers and kids and the principal, Tony Cook, and his successor, Steve Dillon—gave my boy his first chance to live as a normal teenager. When Ryan was feeling okay, he went to games, to proms. People talked to him in the halls He sat on the telephone with his new friends for hours. He got a job at the local skateboard shop and became our resident expert.

Andrea found a whole new gang of buddies. They went out boating on the lake; they hung out at the Dairy Queen. Our lives had stabilized so much that I could now go back to work, and Andrea could now go back to skating. She performed in the opening ceremonies of the Pan Am Games in 1987. I was sewing on sequins again. The sparkle returned.

In the winter of 1987, Governor Orr presented Ryan with a very great honor: one of the Sagamore of the Wabash awards for citizens who have accomplished something special for Indiana. The convocation was held at Hamilton Heights High, which then received the first ever "Spirit of the Heartland" award for welcoming Ryan with such warmth and courtesy. I had finally found a safe place for my children.

Michael Jackson invited us to spend a day at his magical Neverland Ranch. Twenty-seven hundred acres north of Santa Barbara, with a zoo, and an amusement park with a Ferris wheel, and a merry-go-round and bumper cars and spinning rides that turned you upside down, and a video-game arcade, and a movie house which only stocked happy films. Music came out of the gardens.

Michael took us on a tour of the house. He said he wanted to have a family, a boy and a girl. He had their rooms already done up, with dollhouses and model trains.

It was not to be the last time that I would come upon a rich, famous man longing for the comfort of a family of his own.

As one who had also dreamed of perfect dollhouses in a perfect world, I felt a kinship with Michael. I think that one reason he's so popular is that he's in touch with the part of ourselves that we usually keep secret and treasure most—the fantasy part. At the pool, he noticed Ryan leafing through the pages of his favorite car magazine, *Mustang Monthly*. That glimpse into Ryan's dream world was all Michael Jackson needed.

Shortly after we came home, a car salesman from Noblesville called and said, "Ryan White? We've got a red Mustang here for you. It's from Michael Jackson."

Phil Donahue had seen Ryan on the children's program *3-2-1 Contact*, in a show called "I Have AIDS," and he was impressed with the possibilities of educating America's children on a grand scale. He asked Ryan to come and do a show before a live audience full of kids, to answer questions and talk kid-to-kid about his disease. Because of the respect Phil showed him, Ryan now understood that he had not just a cause but a *career*, that he was a national figure and a public servant whose task it was to help his country overcome the plague of AIDS.

He began to plan the rest of his life, and his death, with that in mind.

I know that each of the celebrities who developed close relationships with Ryan did so because he moved them and inspired them. Like the media, they were starved for sincerity, and Ryan was the real article. His suffering was real. His joy and his appreciation of everything they did for him—every toy and T-shirt they sent, every concert and dinner they brought him to—were genuine.

Each of these people gave something of their personal magic to make his burden lighter. I soon stopped thinking of them as celebrities. I thought of them as blessed strangers, messengers of joy.

I thought of them as Ryan's new guardian angels.

Chapter 5

The Sparkle

A child who knows he's going to die wants everything right away. That's natural. He wants to experience every single thing that he can, even if it's dangerous—driving a fast car, jumping off a high diving board, traveling everywhere, meeting everybody. Ryan would sit in his room filled with miniature figures, action heroes, model cars and planes, comic books and autographed photos of rock stars and athletes, images and symbols of all the powerful, active, high-tech lives he couldn't lead, and the small figures would fill him with bigger and bigger dreams. Just like me, imagining paper angels in the grit of the Delco line; just like my mother with her statuettes of pale, holy children, Ryan comforted himself with fantasies.

119

That's all he had, really, those dreams. He put all his strength of mind into touching as many of them as he could in his short time.

Ryan was almost always in a good mood. Even when he was in the hospital, he'd try to give me a smile when I walked in the door. However, sometimes if he couldn't do something—go to some concert, or meet some exciting people, or travel to some interesting place—because he was too sick or too tied up with school, he'd get pouty and upset. Then I might scold him.

"Now, Ryan, you think about what you said. That sounds like a spoiled little kid."

He'd feel contrite and apologize right away. Maybe write me a note or send me a card.

"Mother, please forgive me for treating you so terrible. I honestly wasn't pouting about anything. I'm sorry for being so selfish and stupid. Just remember I love you and always will . . . Your little boy, Ryan."

The sick person would have to be downright saintly never to give in to crankiness. But if you're the one giving care, you can't ever take an angry outburst personally—because it's really the illness speaking or the medication speaking and not the true, loving heart inside.

One day Ryan just grabbed my hand and started swinging it.

"Now, Ryan, when you do something as nice as this, you must want something."

"I don't want anything. Can't a son hold his mother's hand?"

"Come on now, Ryan . . ."

"No, really, Mom. I want to thank you for all you've done. For me. Standing by me like you've done."

No one can ever take those words away from me. No one can ever take away what I felt that day as a mother.

Much as Ryan enjoyed Hamilton Heights High, he couldn't get to class that often during the 1989-90 school year. When he could, he went to school only four hours a day. The school authorities adjusted his classes for that schedule. He loved driving his Mustang to school. That was the pride of his life, that car that Michael had given him.

Kids who didn't know him would sometimes kid him that he wasn't really old enough to drive—because he looked so young. (He got his driver's license at sixteen just like everybody else.) He had never gone through puberty; the disease had hit him just before it started, so he never grew much or got hair on his body. If he went to McDonald's, he had to sit on a pillow.

Very often, he'd wake up full of energy in the morning, take his shower, get dressed, eat a bite of breakfast—and then be too exhausted to go to school.

His nights were hard. Frequently he just couldn't get comfortable or he'd be too cold to sleep, or he'd run a high fever and have a sweat and then it would go away and finally he'd get to sleep.

I'd get up at six-thirty every morning and go in and see if he was sleeping all right. If he was, then I'd have an hour or so of freedom. I'd let the dogs out. And I'd clean my kitchen—wash the floor and run a sinkful of water to wash anything that might be dirty from the day before. Then I'd get his Factor ready. I always liked to get his Factor and his AZT and his antibiotics ready before he woke up.

It took me thirty-five minutes to drive from Cicero to Delco. If Ryan was well enough to attend school, I tried to make the shift that started at 5:48 A.M. and got me off at 2 P.M., because then I could make it home just about the time he did. I could work a full week except for every other Friday, when I needed to go with him to Riley Hospital to get gamma globulin. Sometimes he was sick, and I couldn't work, and I would support us on the money that kindhearted folks had sent us, which I had banked in preparation for just such a time.

Many people have asked me if I ever considered giving up this sporadic time-on time-off system and just quitting my job. The answer is, "Never." I knew an awful lot of folks suffering from AIDS who had been forced to go on welfare because of the colossal expense of having this disease. Delco's insurance plan was such that I never had to do that. We might have needed help, but we weren't completely down and out—and that meant everything to me.

I never hired homemakers or housekeepers or visiting nurses to help me with Ryan. Having a nurse at home would make our pretty yellow house like an extension of the hospital. Ryan would never feel that he wasn't sick. Andrea would never be able to escape from her brother's illness. The feeling of a "normal" life—with a bustling kitchen and phones ringing and the TV blaring—was what I wanted. So I did it all. Housework. Cooking. Driving. Every hour of my day was taken.

I never could seem to put my feet up for five minutes. I was forever mopping the floor, answering mail, making arrangements, doing the dishes. Every Thursday we went to the comic book store because that was when the new ones came in.

Ryan helped me every bit as much as he could. He did his own wash, kept his room clean, changed his own sheets. He took care of his own grooming completely. He was always finicky about his hair and real picky about his clothes. The more he was out of school, the more he wanted to look like he was *in* school, to be just like all the other kids.

If he couldn't get to school, he'd go down to the basement, where we kept all his magazines—every car magazine you could imagine—and soon he'd be calling me: "Mom, when are you coming down?" I'd join him and just sit, working puzzles, painting Christmas ornaments or doing some other kind of crafts, reading my garden magazines, anything to be there with him. Or I'd clean the house and he'd be sitting close by, telling me about some new thing he was going to do to his car, and I'd say, "Yes, hon, that sure sounds grand . . ." when, truthfully, I didn't have the faintest idea what he was talking about.

Sometimes he'd go out for a bit, just drive around in his car, and that would revive him and lift his spirits, to know he could get out and drive his car. It just broke my heart to see Ryan being so thrilled about something so simple. He'd come back after maybe half an hour and be so exhausted that he would have to lie down.

I didn't do much of anything for myself. Hardly ever got my hair done or bought a dress. The truth is, I forgot how I looked in those last months. My whole life was spent taking care of him and, when we could manage it, keeping up with Andrea's skating. What saved me was my friends Mary Baker and Betsy Stewart.

Mary Baker is a heart of gold. There isn't anybody in this world she wouldn't help. You didn't dare tell Mary that you liked something or you needed something, because she'd go right out and get it. Betsy Stewart is a real pretty blond woman, full of energy and good spirits. She'd always have something positive to say, something uplifting to show me, or a good story to tell. Sometimes if Ryan was strong enough to go to school, I'd be able to spend an hour with one of these women. We'd go out and have breakfast, or go to the plant nursery or the Hallmark store. That was the only time when I could take my mind off Ryan's illness.

At one point during 1988, Ryan developed a stomach infection. He was in the hospital for close to two months, retching and vomiting everything he ate. He so didn't want a feeding tube—but at last Dr. Kleiman told him he simply had to have it or he would starve to death.

I stopped working and stayed with him as much as I could. I slept in a chair that made up into a bed at night. But the truth is, I could hardly sleep just for listening to him breathe. He had several diabetic seizures during that time. They made him blind. He nearly died. He recovered . . . but after those two months in the hospital, there was a new weariness about Ryan and a grave, deliberate kind of maturity.

·

The nightmare of AIDS is that it brings you one powerful infection after another. I thought every cough, every fever might be his last. With AIDS, you never know whether a symptom is serious or mild. The patient is sick and then gets well, and no sooner does he get well than he gets sick again.

It is exactly the same for the caregiver. No sooner do you sit down and take a breath and sleep through a night than the sleepless nights return.

It is the same for your hopes. They go out like candles, and then they burn again, and then they die down. Again.

Educating the public about AIDS became Ryan's life, his career. In between bouts of illness, he spoke at Boys Town in Nebraska, at the National Education Association in New Orleans. During one trip to Washington, in which he was interviewed for *Nightline* and spoke before the President's Commission on AIDS, he and his friend Jill Stewart (Betsy's daughter) went sightseeing and had a ball.

Ryan was light. Thin. Still, transporting him through airports sometimes felt like dragging a load of rocks. I groaned with the effort it took for him to put one foot in front of the other. Other times he'd feel wonderful and race through the streets with the rest of us trundling along behind.

During 1989, Delco allowed me to take an unpaid leave of absence, at the request of the State Board of Health. I was helping Dr. Myers and his staff create some information programs, and Ryan was making a series of extremely effective public-service announcements. Ryan was plagued with infections. But he did the PSAs anyway.

The first one aired in November of 1989. There he was, with his direct, honest gaze, talking to kids. "Hello, I'm Ryan White," he said. "You know, as much as we've talked to you about AIDS, a lot of you still aren't listening. Today is World AIDS Day, so please listen. I didn't have a choice when I got AIDS. You do. If someone's feeding you a line, trying to get you to have sex or do drugs, before you do something stupid, pick up the phone and call the Indiana AIDS hot line. Let's work together to beat AIDS."

Right after Christmas, Michael Jackson invited him to come out to California. Michael was getting things set up so that children who were sick could come out to the ranch and enjoy themselves. Dr. Kleiman and I were completely reassured that there were enough medical personnel around to take care of any emergency.

I sent Ryan off to California. Even though it was warm out there, he needed his heater. He was so cold that Michael got him an extra-heavy coat.

People have asked me if I ever hesitated sending Ryan off alone to stay with Michael Jackson. The answer is: *Not for one minute.*

Down the block from us, there was a family named Ginder whose kids often played with Andrea. The father, Roy, was as much of a nut about cars as Ryan. On a nice day he could be seen in his driveway, working for hours to rebuild an old '57 Chevy. Ryan would go down there and just watch and talk a little.

"If you look at the car as a whole," Roy said, "it will disappoint you. But if you look at the little pieces, one piece at a time, and just fix each piece separately, then before long, you'll have the whole puzzle put together and the car will be fixed."

Roy Ginder helped Ryan add all kinds of things to the Mustang. He wanted to add features to the gorgeous car that would make it look more like a Saleen, which I had never heard of, but which was apparently a fabulous car that had been named for its inventor. Ryan wanted new tires. And hubcaps painted the exact red of the car body. And ground effects, which are gadgets that lower the actual body of the car without moving the suspension, much like the air foils you see on racing cars. He wanted a big engraving on the rear window that said "Faster than a Heartbeat."

"Mr. Ginder is just totally the greatest guy, Mom," he said after one of their grease-monkey sessions. I protested that maybe Ryan was bothering our neighbor. However, Roy said that if the boy had the money to pay for these axles and spindles and whatever, he'd be glad to help him out and install them. They spun some dreams about Ryan possibly coming on as an apprentice in the body shop where Roy was working. In fact, they even did a little drag racing in some secret spot near Cicero—Roy in his souped-up '57 Chevy and Ryan in his scarlet Mustang.

Luckily for both of them, I didn't find that out until much later.

His friendship with Roy Ginder meant much more to Ryan than shop talk about cars. It meant entrance into the technical world of machines, the grown-up world of dirty hands and heavy work. It felt like being a man.

In the summer of 1989, Ryan rode through downtown Cicero

as Honorary Grand Marshal of the Fourth of July parade. He was smiling and waving. It was a hot day—but when he came home, he said he was feeling real cold.

I tried so hard not to abandon Andrea during this long period of decline. We gave her a big sixteenth birthday party at Pizza Hut with all her new friends from Cicero. Somebody gave her this great sweatshirt of the hunks from Chippendale's, and Ryan posed for a picture with his new friend Steffonie Garland. In November 1989, Andrea went to the Olympic Training Center in Colorado Springs, in the shadow of the towering mountains, to practice with the other girls. Maybe roller-skating did not win a spot on the Olympic calendar . . . but the joy of being there with all those other kids, away from me and Ryan and AIDS—that was worth everything.

In September 1989, we went to the Emmy Awards. Our show, *I Have Aids—a Teenager's Story: a 3-2-1 Contact Extra*, produced by Al Hyslop and Susan Lynn Schwartz for PBS and the Children's Television Workshop, was up against *Free to Be . . . a Family*, produced by Marlo Thomas and Christopher Cerf and Robert Dalrymple for ABC in association with Gostelradio (Soviet TV). We lost to Marlo's show, but we felt like we were losing to friends who had the same values and the same agenda that we had: to make this world safer for children.

Ryan looked kind of beat, sitting there in front of all that heavy food, in the glare of those celebrity lights, and Phil Donahue saw that.

"How you doing, buddy?"

"Okay, Phil. Just fine."

"How about you and me skipping out of here and getting some burgers?"

"Great!"

So off they went, Phil Donahue and Ryan White, to have fast food while the rest of us did our Emmy thing. That was "pure Phil"—that amazing ability to cut through all the glamour and the glitz and see what a real kid really needed.

In the fall of 1989, Ryan began to have terrible trouble with a hernia—a torn groin muscle which he had contracted from coughing. It often prevented him from urinating easily. Coupled with growing liver dysfunction, it made his life just miserable.

It got so bad, we decided he simply had to have an operation to repair it. For most men, this is a simple procedure, requiring no overnight hospital stay. For Ryan, because of his hemophilia, it was life-threatening. We waited months and months for them to do the operation.

At last we checked into Riley. Ryan was all prepped and ready to go. We waited and waited, wondering why they hadn't yet commenced the operation, what was taking them so long. Dr. Kleiman said they were doing blood work, waiting for tests to come back. We waited and waited some more. Finally Dr. Kleiman reported that Ryan's blood-platelet count was so low, the surgery could not be safely performed.

I knew we were in serious trouble then. If they couldn't operate on his hernia, that meant they couldn't do anymore for him. For the first time, Ryan began to feel as though his time was running out. Before, he had been sick and then he'd get better, but now he wasn't getting better.

Andrea couldn't accept that. "Ryan will get better," she said. "You listen to me, Mom. Ryan will get better."

Ryan himself had begun to think differently about the future now. *People* magazine had called, wanting to buy the exclusive rights to be the only publication allowed in to see him and be with our family if it looked like Ryan wasn't going to make it.

"I can't allow you to sell those rights," I told Ryan. "It'll feel like you are selling your life . . . and I don't want you to die, I want you to keep fighting . . . I don't want people to think you've given up."

"It's about time we stopped worrying what other people think, Mom," he said gently. "This way I know you and Andrea will be taken care of."

"No, Ryan . . ."

"Mom," he said, "I'll sign the papers. I want Bill Shaw to do the story and Taro to take the pictures. I know Taro would never take a picture of me that I would not want taken."

He smiled and held my hand and went ahead and sold the rights. He was thinking like a man, trying to take care of his sister and his mom, and buying himself an insurance policy.

The good wishes of the world sustained us. Kids who had seen Ryan on *Donahue* wrote him constantly, diverting him with their requests for advice. The children of Northview Middle School made a thousand paper cranes in Ryan's honor, following the example of Japanese students who had folded a thousand paper cranes for a classmate sick with leukemia. In the winter of 1990, Ryan received a gold statue from the National Mickey Mouse Club for "children who make a difference." We tried twice to make the trip to those awards, but we never got there because Ryan was too ill.

He had thrush infections in his mouth that made it impossible for him to swallow. He craved the warmth of the sun, but he broke out in horrible hives if it came in direct contact with his skin. He was plagued by shingles. I would change the bandages constantly.

Hopelessness was hitting us for the first time. I saw it in Ryan, and he saw it in me. He needed a tremendous infusion of protein to keep up his strength. Dr. Kleiman suggested that we bypass his wrecked digestive system and once again put him on a feeding tube. Ryan absolutely refused. I know now, with hindsight, that he was so sick by then that Dr. Kleiman was reluctant to do anything that would cause him more pain. So he allowed us to go home from Riley with gallons of this horrible protein drink, with orders that Ryan had to take it seven times a day.

How Ryan hated that stuff! I tried mixing it with orange juice, with milk, anything to get him to drink it—but when he saw me coming with it, he'd just snarl. So now I became the enemy, chasing him around the house with a cup.

Ryan sat on the edge of his bed in his fun-filled, gadget-filled, fantasy-filled room, no longer able to find comfort in it. "I'm so tired of being sick," he said.

I was tired, too—I wouldn't be honest if I didn't say that. It is the hardest thing for me to live with now, the memory of those moments when I became so depressed and hopeless from seeing him suffer that I didn't think I could stand it one more minute. You feel that as a mom, you should be able to carry the world for your children. How shall I ever forgive myself for those few moments when the world grew too heavy?

We were both so sick of his being sick. It all whirled around us, this feeling of helplessness. I'd keep praying and praying: "Please come out with a cure, find a cure before the time runs out . . ." but I knew in my heart the time had already run out. And still, I didn't want to give up. I didn't dare give up.

Ryan had his own vision one night, when he was back in the hospital with a lung infection and they had to put him on the respirator. He said that the Lord had come to him and given him a preview of Heaven. "I'm not afraid anymore, Mom," he kept saying. "I know I'm going to a better place."

It was March 1990. We had been invited to Los Angeles for a big Oscar party sponsored by Athletes and Entertainers for Kids, a wonderful organization run by Elise Kim. President Ronald Reagan and Mrs. Reagan were going to be at the party. Ryan wanted very much to go, especially since President Reagan had never acknowledged AIDs while he was in the White House, and Ryan had learned, as I had, that the leadership of the politicians was crucial when it came to any health issue. The plan was to go to L.A., come home, then catch a plane to Miami, where Stanley Hubbard of Hubbard Broadcasting was sending the three of us for spring break.

Ryan did a photo shoot for *People* magazine, becoming one of the year's "Fifty most beautiful people." Matt Frewer showed us his new house and his new puppies. On March 26, in Beverly Hills, under a huge tent, we attended a benefit in memory of Ruth Berle, Milton's Berle's late wife. My Andrea looked gorgeous in a strapless black sequined dress. But Ryan looked pale; his smile was weak. At the Oscar party for kids at the Beverly Wilshire, he met the Reagans and Sara Gilbert from *Roseanne* and Danny Pintauro from *Who's the Boss?* He had his picture taken with J.D. Roth.

Mrs. Reagan did not let go of his hand the whole time they were together. She knew how bad he was. She whispered to me: "He's not doing well. I can tell." A mom can always tell.

The next morning, Ryan didn't feel well enough even to go out. His face had swelled up. And he had that wispy wet cough again. He made an appearance with his friend Howie Long of the L.A. Raiders on *The Home Show*, but you could see he wasn't up to it. I have a picture of him and Howie on the air together, and the look of worry on Howie's face tells it all.

We flew back to Indiana in the middle of the night on March 29 and checked right into Riley. Ryan had a severe respiratory infection. For the first three days, they gave him oxygen. He was different this time, more frightened. He didn't want me to leave the room. So I stayed there at his bedside.

Mary Baker and Betsy Stewart came as soon as they heard Ryan was in the hospital. He had fallen asleep. They were waiting downstairs. I thought I would just run down and say hi and thank them for coming and then get back before he woke up. When I heard myself paged over the loudspeakers, I thought, *Oh, my goodness, Ryan woke up and I wasn't there and he's throwing a fit! He wants me!*

It wasn't that. It was that Ryan had taken a terrible turn for the worse, and the nurses and doctors were moving him into intensive care to try and save his life.

I don't know how the media found out that Ryan White was probably facing his last battle, but they did, they *always* find out, and in no time it was on the news. Suddenly thousands of people began calling the hospital with prayers and wishes for his recovery. I felt like each of those people who called was a kind of angel, that together they formed this chorus of angels praying for my boy.

Elton came right away. His people were real upset because he had to attend a press conference about his new album, and they wanted him to just look in on us and then return immediately to L.A. But when he talked to Dr. Kleiman and realized how serious it was, he just held my hand and said, "I'm not leaving you. I don't care what happens. I'm going to be here for you."

Every single day, from early in the morning to late at night, that man was at the hospital. He talked to the doctors, to my poor, frightened mother and father. He distracted Andrea with jokes and stories. Whatever I needed, he made sure I got it. During that last week and a half, my leaning torch was Elton John.

The press began arriving with trucks and equipment, needing information, parking spaces, hotel accommodations, fax machines, electrical cables, food. And some of them weren't always so polite in their dealings with the hospital and the citizens of Indianapolis.

Mary Maxwell, who worked in public relations at the Indiana University Medical Center, suggested that our old friend Carrie Jackson Van Dyke should serve as a liaison between the hospital and me, and become the press spokesperson for our family. David McCarty, Carrie's boss at the State Board of Health and the producer of Ryan's PSAs, immediately gave her leave to do so.

Carrie's presence comforted me immeasurably. She announced the rules of the game. She said to the press, "We're going to do everything we can for you, but you must realize that Ryan is a patient and his privacy must be guarded." The hospital set up news briefings about Ryan's condition twice a day, at ten and four, so they could all make the twelve o'clock and six o'clock news programs. By ten o'clock at night, all visitors had to be out of the hospital, except for those members of his family staying over.

Phil Donahue understood that despite the media attention we had received, I was still an inexperienced person. So he flew out from New York, determined that nobody should take advantage of me. He consulted constantly with Elton about the arrangements. Thousands of calls were coming in. The mail piled up, good wishes from everywhere. Flowers. Get-well balloons. I was completely cut off from all this flurry and confusion, living between Ryan's bedside and the waiting room where my family hung out, pacing the corridors with Andrea when the nurses tossed us out because Ryan was having some treatment. I knew that out there, Carrie and Mary and their staff were taking care of everything—but I didn't really know how much of everything there was. Until one day, after almost a week, I allowed Elton to convince me that the media needed to hear from me and that I had to go down and meet the press.

Andrea stood right beside me. I have no idea what I said. All I can remember is this blur of faces, the bounce of my voice in the microphones.

I told Carrie, "I can't do this again. Please, don't ask me to do this again."

And she put her arms around me and took me back inside.

Not all the reporters were content to receive the news that was being given out. They would sneak into the hospital, try any trick to get up to see Ryan. Elton arrived and hired Papa Bear and his company, Elite Security Services, to guard Ryan and our family, and also incidentally to stand guard over the famous people who were coming to see him.

The traffic of visitors and press people and just plain curiosity seekers so distressed the nurses and the other patients that the hospital decided to put Ryan in a room in the back, out of the way. People kept trying to photograph him—not just the press but regular people with their own little cameras, the hospital staff even, just trying to get a glimpse of this dying kid who had achieved such a strange sort of fame.

Ryan fell into a coma—induced by all the sedatives and painkillers they had to give him so his body would accept the equipment they needed to put into him to keep him alive. That is such a crazy thing in medicine these days, when the side effect of the treatment that keeps you alive is that you become comatose. It's a kind of insanity that many people with desperately ill loved ones face in hospitals all the time. I kept waiting for Ryan to wake up. I called to him. I sat by his bedside and held his hand and called to him and told him that I loved him, over and over and over again. But he didn't hear me.

Elton arranged for me and Andrea to stay on the floor in some doctors' quarters so we wouldn't have to go down and face the media. Flowers came to us from everywhere. Hundreds and hundreds of beautiful bouquets were lined up against the walls, the brightness of their colors wasted on us. Elton made sure we knew who had sent them, that we had a complete record of every rose and daisy, and then he arranged for them to be taken out as fast as they came in, sent off to other patients' room and nursing homes, where they could be enjoyed.

Then Elton got it into his head that music might revive Ryan and that what he really needed was a good stereo. So he went out and bought one, along with a whole slew of Bruce Springsteen and Michael Jackson tapes.

"Why didn't you bring any of yours?" I asked.

"Oh, Ryan likes Bruce and Michael," he answered. "He doesn't want to listen to me."

It tickled me so, this big star suddenly getting all bashful about pushing his own songs. Believe me, Ryan would have wanted to hear Elton John.

I sat by my boy's bedside and held his hand, which had grown so swollen. When I thought I would faint, Elton hugged me. When I cried, he cried with me. He really became part of our family in those terrible days.

With all the tubes and the machines and the monitoring devices, and now the stereo, there wasn't room for anything else in that room with Ryan. But Elton said, "You know, when he wakes up, I want this room to be *decorated*. The kids at all these schools have sent so many beautiful banners wishing him well. Let's hang them, so when he gets better, he'll know how much everyone cared about him."

The hospital staff must have thought we were insane. Here's this comatose kid, on life support, with a half-crazy mother calling his name, trying to talk to him while he sleeps. He probably can't hear a thing, but Elton buys him music. He can't see a thing, but Elton gets hold of one of the doctors, and the two of them are standing precariously on chairs, hanging decorative posters and banners on the walls above the screens and the wires and the bleeping monitors.

I stood there watching Ryan's thin little body swell more and more. I knew there was nothing more anybody could do. Before he drifted into unconsciousness, Ryan had told me, "If you think there's a chance, Mom, go for it." We did. Until the last second, we went for everything we could. I still have the notes he wrote to us, assenting to the use of the respirator . . . the last little notes.

I leaned down close to him and whispered, "It's okay, son. You can let go."

Then he died. They revived him for a few minutes. In this case, "reviving" meant that they couldn't ever wake him up, but they could get his heart going by mechanical means. Momentarily he would die again; I knew that perfectly well. I knew there was no chance. But still, to have to call the battle lost . . . it was a moment of inexpressible sorrow for me and my family.

"If you want, you can tell them no more," Elton said. "It's up to you, Jeanne."

I talked to my parents, to Andrea. Then I told the doctors, "No more."

Marty Kleiman, who had taken care of Ryan from the beginning, who had helped him live for almost six years when other physicians had predicted that he would die in six months, went out and made the announcement that my boy had passed away in his sleep, without pain.

The sparkle was gone.

I remember Carrie Jackson Van Dyke once asked me, "How do you live, Jeanne, day to day, knowing that your son is going to die?"

And I had answered, "We don't think about death in this house. We don't have time for it. If you allow it into your life, it will eat you up. You have to go on with your life, making the most of every day and every hour."

Chapter 6

One Piece at a Time

No matter how much time passes, death is so hard to accept. You have all these questions within yourself. Does my son see me as I go about my daily life? Can he really look down and see me and know what's going on? Does he really know what we are thinking? Will he recognize us when we get to Heaven? Does he see me decorate his grave? Has he met the others who have followed him? Are they together? You wonder all that, all the time.

Most of the time I think: Yes, I believe I'll see him again, hug him again and hold his hand. I'll look up from my sewing and he'll be there. That's what keeps me going, that I really believe that. But I still want *somebody to tell me, definitely, that this is the way it's going to be. Sometimes I feel like I can't wait until I die—because I'm so sure I'm going to know something after I die that I can't know for certain now.*

I have the hardest time when I visit Ryan's grave. I can fix it and plant it and clean it and arrange it, and laugh over the stuff that kids have left there, and I'm fine. But if I try to talk to Ryan, the tears just start flowing.

There's so many things you want to say—and you just can't . . . and you just can't bear it. I look at the beautiful stone and I feel terrible emptiness in my heart.

In the wake of Ryan's death, I felt that I was in pieces, a dilapidated old wreck like one of those cars that my neighbor Roy Ginder used to rebuild in his driveway. I had worn an old, ill-fitting dress to the funeral. Most of the stuff in my closet was like that. Andrea watched me sitting around the house, looking just a mess, and she suggested gently that I start paying some attention to my appearance again and go out and get some new stuff to wear. It seemed an impossible task. I simply did not have the strength to put myself back together after so much tragedy.

My family could not really comfort me. They could only endure in their love and wait for better days. I tried to dodge the worry in my mother's eyes.

An insightful little book by Sarah Rich Wheeler and Margaret M. Pike, for which I wrote the introduction, accurately portrayed the troubles of families who have lost children. The authors perfectly captured the way my mom in particular felt about me. Her despair. Her inability to make me whole again. "I can't kiss the hurt and make it go away," they wrote in the voice of all grandmothers. "I can't even kiss a small part of it away. There is no bandage large enough to cover her bleeding heart."

I think now that I could never have healed myself. If the pieces of my life reassembled after my son passed away, it was because of the love and concern and strength of other people, members of my family patiently waiting for their powerless time to end, and perfect strangers just reaching out.

I received sixty thousand letters. Sixty thousand.

People sent letters to the church, to Riley Hospital, to my home, to Hamilton Heights High School, to the bank. Phil Donahue took some of the letters back to New York with him. He called me from there, all excited.

"Jeanne! Do you realize—almost all of this mail is from kids! We've got to do something about these letters. These kids were really fascinated by Ryan; he's a hero and an idol to them."

"He was a sick boy, Phil . . . he never could answer all the mail he got . . . and it made him real unhappy to answer some and not all."

"I think it's important to answer this mail, Jeanne."

"I can't now . . . I just can't . . . I haven't got the strength . . ."

"I understand. What I'm going to do is get you some help. We'll set up an account and we'll get you an assistant."

"Please, Phil, I don't think I can do this."

"I know you're hurting. I know you're grieving. But this boy of yours left a legacy, Jeanne, and you've got to stay involved, for his sake . . ."

Phil Donahue had always possessed a sense of history about the AIDS crisis and Ryan's role in it. His talk show was the one that ran the earliest program on AIDS back in 1982. He believed that AIDS was going to be stopped only if young people could be made

140

aware of the danger it posed. He focused on kids, on families. In his own family, he had tremendous support for this way of thinking from his late father-in-law, Danny Thomas, who had started St. Jude Children's Research Hospital in Memphis, the leading institution in the country for children with catastrophic disease. Phil's wife, Marlo, had inherited her father's passionate interest in St. Jude's and devoted much of her career as an actress and producer to creating great shows for kids like *Free to Be You and Me*. A publicist who worked for Phil at that time, Karin Lippert, became a very close friend and adviser to me. She had had tragedies in her own life, and knew as I did what the pressures were on the caregiver, how expensive American medicine was, how important it was to reach out and help families.

It was Phil who kept calling me, urging me to respond to Senators Kennedy and Hatch and go to Washington to help lobby on the Ryan White CARE Act. Once I had made that trip to Washington, wet my feet in the corridors of the Capitol, he was convinced I had a new career ahead of me as an advocate in AIDS education.

I wasn't at all sure about that. The deluge of invitations to make speeches scared me silly. I had managed to say a few paragraphs here and there on TV shows, at press conferences, but the idea of standing up in front of a large audience and giving a prepared address seemed totally impossible. Phil insisted that I could do it. However, I had no public or business skills. Just the act of having to write formal, intelligent-sounding letters to members of Congress had exhausted me; I had never conducted a correspondence about important ideas with important people. What if I said something wrong that would then be on the record for all time? The Ryan White CARE Act supporters told me not to worry, just to write the way I spoke, like a mom and a plain person. But this piece of myself that was supposed to feel confident about public activity was sure hard to find.

In an effort to help me with the masses of mail, Marlo contacted somebody in Indianapolis who had worked on the St. Jude's telethon and asked her to recommend a person in the Cicero area who had secretarial skills. The networking led her to a pretty blue-eyed woman named Shelley Henson.

Shelley was just like me, a mom juggling a million obligations. She had incredible stamina and an open mind, the two most important qualifications for the job. She adjusted quietly and quickly.

We set up an office in the basement of my house, and Shelley came to work there every day. She kept track of all the phone calls, sliced through the mail. But it still seemed like we weren't getting anywhere. The letters just kept coming. On one given day, the post office had seven boxes of mail for us. Two girls who had been Ryan's friends at Hamilton Heights High spent the summer helping us. We had little hearts made up that said, "Ryan White thanks you from the heart. 1971-1990." We sent out thousands.

Imperceptibly, I began to feel more at ease with this activity. I just got used to it, like cooking or ironing; it felt like another household chore I was pretty good at. The public piece of my life was beginning to take shape.

I had been accustomed to filling every minute of the day with busy tasks that centered on Ryan. Now, with some of my time occupied once again, I searched for a way to fill the rest of it . . . particularly the hours when I was alone and grief weighed heavily.

And once again I thought of the dollhouse.

I had always dreamed of having a big dollhouse, since I was a little girl. I wanted one so I could decorate it and fix it up and make it the home that I fantasized about having one day. I never thought I'd have that home for real—so the dollhouse was my substitute, it captured my imagination.

When we used to go to Lafayette, Indiana, to see our lawyer, Mr. Vaughan, there was a certain fork in the road we'd always come to, and right at that fork stood this big dollhouse store. In the windows they'd have gorgeous, custom-made dollhouses with many rooms filled with tiny people and tiny furniture. They had a house that looked like the one the Waltons lived in on the TV show that I had always enjoyed so much. They had a big Victorian country farmhouse. I'd slow down the car and take a long look—but I'd never actually stop, because we were almost always running late and Mr. Vaughan was waiting and we had so much vital stuff to worry about.

Ryan knew how that store excited me. He always said, "If ever I can make some money, Mom, I'm going to give you some and send you in there to buy yourself the dollhouse you've always wanted."

I answered, "Sure, honey, that'll be great," never dreaming that his resolution would come true.

But then it happened. Ryan did make some money for his movie. And as we were heading out to Lafayette one day, he said, "Okay, Mom, today we're going to stop at that dollhouse place." His eyes were shining. He was feeling the same pleasure I used to feel bringing my mom a little present from the candy store, the anticipation of seeing a loved one's face about to light up with delight.

To our disappointment, the dollhouse store was closed. They had gone out of business. So I never did get my dollhouse while Ryan was alive.

When he died, and I was needing something to distract me, I thought of the dollhouse again and started looking. A little store in

Noblesville sold a beautiful log-cabin-type dollhouse, but it was kind of small. I called the owner and asked if he could make me a bigger one, with several floors. He made it just perfect—three rooms and a bathroom upstairs, and downstairs a kitchen and a living room.

The time that I would have spent sitting with Ryan, watching TV with him, preparing his medicine and his dozens of tiny meals— that time I now filled with a wild burst of energy, miniaturizing every single detail of our lives so that I could always see us as we were. I'd take pictures of my pictures of my family so they would come out real little, and then I'd put them in tiny frames and set them out on tiny dressers. I took pictures of the magazines which had featured articles on Ryan and made them into tiny magazines and put them in tiny magazine racks. I took pictures of the yard from our windows and hung them up on the outside of the dollhouse windows so the view from inside would be the same as our real view. I made a tiny scrapbook, tiny braided rugs. Out front, I set a miniature of our dog Wally's little house, and added garden statuary like folks in our neighborhood have—a little bear, a little squirrel. By the side of the fireplace I set a stack of tiny logs. There was a grandma in the house and a grandpa reading the Indianapolis newspaper. In the dining room I placed a miniature Christmas tree with tiny presents under it. I even made a little tiny setting of Gizzy, my newest dog, going to the bathroom on newspaper in the kitchen. I found an adorable little-girl miniature that looked like Andrea and set her out like she was playing in the yard, and a little-boy miniature that I dressed to look like Ryan in his pajamas, upstairs in his bedroom. I actually found a little gorilla that reminded me of Ryan's big stuffed gorilla, George. Eventually I did up the mom's bedroom with linens in a black-and-red-flowered print, much like the beautiful quilts and sheets and pillow shams that Marlo had sent as a gift to cheer me up after Ryan died.

That dollhouse was my way of perfecting things. I had complete control there, and didn't have to hear opinions from anybody. I could plan it, dream it, arrange it any way I wanted. Nothing had to be there. Anything could be there. For a woman who had been presented with one terrible inevitability after another, it was a little bit of paradise.

Phil and Marlo invited me and Andrea and a couple of her friends to visit their home by the sea in Connecticut. In the sunny, breezy house, I relaxed a little and tried to collect my thoughts about the future.

Phil wanted me to start a foundation to teach young people about AIDS. He introduced me to his friend, Ralph Nader, who suggested that I sign on with a speakers' bureau he recommended. In fact, I had already been contacted by the Keppler Agency, which had become interested in taking me on after they heard me at a press conference in Washington. After my visit to Connecticut, I realized that many important people like Ralph made their speaking engagements through agencies, and I told Keppler I would think about it.

I came home refreshed, feeling a little more clear-headed.

Phil's idea about a foundation was sounding more and more sensible. He offered the help of his lawyers—Rich Heller and others at Frankfurt, Garbus, Klein and Selz—to start setting up the legal and financial underpinnings that a foundation would need. Their efforts came none too soon.

One day a man from Boston called and told Shelley that some folks had come to him asking for money for the Ryan White Foundation. He had given them $5,000. Then, to his surprise, they showed up again a few months later, wanting more money. He was just checking to see whether we had ever received the money or if we had ever heard of these people.

Well, of course we hadn't. These swindlers had just bold as you please started an account in Ryan's name, and nobody had said they couldn't, and the poor man—and Heaven only knows how many others—had been ripped off by a horrid scheme to take advantage of his kind heart and Ryan's good reputation.

The folks at the Atlanta office of Coca-Cola were more suspicious from the start. Coca-Cola had always been very generous to Ryan and his cause, and they would have known if there was a Ryan White Foundation because we would have told them first off. So when two men and a woman walked into their Atlanta office and said they represented us and wanted a grant of $10,000, the Coke folks excused themselves and went into another room and called me.

We said that there was no Ryan White Foundation as yet, and the would-be swindlers were caught red-handed.

Then someone called from California and told us Ryan's picture had shown up on some awful AIDS trading cards. I remember one of them was so tasteless that it featured both Kimberly Bergalis and the dentist whom she had accused of infecting her. Ryan's picture was packed with a condom! I couldn't believe it. This company was just printing these cards, using any well-known face they wanted without asking or seeking permission, and selling them as novelty items. They said that all the money from the sale of these cards was going to "an AIDS organization"—but when we called to inquire which one, we never got an answer.

California has very strong laws to prevent the exploitation of famous people. So we filled out papers to make sure that in the

In the beginning…Jeanne Hale, age 4.

And now…Jeanne White educates people about AIDS.

Ryan in seventh grade, age 13.

Ryan at age 16.
(Courtesy of Dennis Gates, Inter-State Studio of Indiana, Inc.)

Ryan as I like to remember him, looking healthy and happy.

Ryan and Andrea were always close.

Andrea and I share a nice moment.

Andrea, Ryan, and his girlfriend, Heather.

Michael Jackson was very generous to Ryan—
here we are at President Clinton's inauguration in 1993.

Elton John will always hold a dear place in my heart.
He looked out for Andrea, too, here in 1995.

Roy and I visit Phil Donahue in his office at "The Donahue Show."

Greg Louganis was both a friend and an inspiration to Ryan.

The AIDS Quilt:
Ryan's square was made by Iredell Middle School,
where "The Ryan White Story" was filmed.

Ryan's memorial.

Judith Light (who played me in
"The Ryan White Story") and
me at the Angel Awards, 1994.

Roy and I got married in a wonderful service on August 1, 1992.

I'm still just a mom.

President Clinton reauthorized the Ryan White Care Act in 1996.
(Courtesy of The White House)

future, Ryan's name and face would be protected from similar kinds of misuse.

In addition to protecting ourselves against all these flimflam scammers, we also needed a foundation to help organize and protect the really wonderful people who wanted to use Ryan's memory for bona fide charitable purposes. Our earliest executive director, Karen Engledow, who was now sitting with me and Shelley and Ryan's friends in the ever-more-crowded basement, established a connection between the cause of AIDS education and the Junior League of Indianapolis. She set up a meeting with these hardworking, charitable women who devote themselves to good works, particularly those affecting young people, in every major city. I went and talked to them, told them that although we had many well-publicized celebrity connections, we did not have anywhere near enough funding to get an effective information campaign off the ground. There was no way that our little basement office could be dismantled, as we had originally planned. In fact, it had to be expanded, and soon, too, before we busted out the sliding glass doors. The Junior League approved a large initial grant and became a major support for our new foundation. Along with that grant, we received not only money but dedicated volunteers who made it their business to devote a couple of days every week to our work. Kathy Harrison and Melinda Taylor, members of that original committee which funded us, are now members of our board.

Meanwhile, the mail—which was supposed to have been finished by now—kept coming. The requests poured in—for pictures and tapes of Ryan, for information about AIDS that would be written in language that teens and preteens could understand. And these people out there in America, they also wanted me—to make an appearance, to make a speech, to kick off a fund-raising drive, to participate in a panel, to counsel a parents' group. They couldn't have Ryan, so they wanted me. And I had a choice—either to ignore all this demand and try to return to my old little private life, or to pull myself together and go out there and try to be the leader everybody seemed to want me to be.

I talked to my friends. Shelley, Mary, Betsy. They were for it. They said it would do me good to be appreciated in my own right.

I talked to my daughter. Andrea was against it. She felt that if I went to work in AIDS education, our family would be engulfed by the disease once more; we'd just be living AIDS forever and ever and always.

I talked to Phil Donahue. He said the demand was too great and that I really didn't have a choice at all.

His confidence got to me. I tried to reassure Andrea that AIDS education would just be a job for me, that I would leave it at the office when I came home, that it wouldn't bleed over into our private lives. I don't think she believed me for a minute, but she smiled and said, "Well, okay, Mom, if you really think you can do that."

Nobody knows how to grieve, not really. It's not a skill you can pass on through the generations. Nobody can teach you how to express your anger and frustration without somehow wounding others, or how to forgive yourself for living on.

Folks had always called us, from the moment Ryan became a media subject. They called for advice, for consolation, with ideas for cures. But after he died, the phone calls became constant. People would call every single day, at all hours, desperate to talk. Somehow, in their minds, I had now become the resident expert in American tragedy. I had already lost my child, and since he was one of the first, those who waited for the same fate to befall their loved ones felt that I could somehow give *them* advice and consolation, or even ideas for cures. They would get my number from somebody in the media, or from a friend who knew somebody in the media who had a colleague who had once done a story on us. If I changed the number or made it unlisted, they would find me anyway.

If they asked for Andrea, she rarely took the call. She insisted on defending herself against any more heartbreak and would happily have done the same for me.

But I couldn't help myself. I kept telling her, "Andrea, hon, what am I supposed to say to these folks? 'I'm too involved in my grief to have time for yours'? I have to talk to them."

Some of these tragedies were so huge that you couldn't get your mind to absorb them. I don't think Americans understand to this day the slaughter that occurred in hemophiliac families. One little girl said she was calling for her aunt, who really needed to talk to me. This poor woman was losing both of her brothers to AIDS— and both of her sons. Another woman was watching three hemophiliac sons die. A woman who had been married to a man who got the disease from a blood transfusion had watched him go and was now dying herself, living her last years in fear that her kids would soon test positive as well. One woman in Seattle told me that her three sons and her sister's two were all HIV-positive. These people would just talk and talk all night long, and I would listen. They would want me to have all the answers. And, of course, I didn't have any.

Everybody wanted to know how long: *How long do I have to live? How long does he or she have to live?* I had been just the same way. It must have driven Dr. Kleiman crazy. You keep asking how long because if they have a year or two, maybe you can dare to hope for a cure, but if they have only a month, maybe you should call the family and arrange the funeral. We all need to try to make sensible arrangements, to try to have a logical life even in the presence of illogical tragedy.

Everybody talked about T-cells. The T-cell count obsesses people with AIDS in the family. But Ryan's life provided proof that sometimes the T-cell count doesn't mean as much as it's supposed to. His T-cell count was so low he shouldn't even have been alive, and yet he was enjoying life. I tried to give people hope. But then, of course, I didn't want to give them false hope.

I know, furthermore, that they were calling me because they were in a panic mode and afraid to call the doctor all the time. I understood that, because I had been there in that exact place. I wanted to call Dr. Kleiman over every cough, every fever, and I couldn't, so I would sit awake half the night, biting my tongue.

With hindsight, I understood that many of these people were looking to me for something I would have given anything to possess when I was back in Kokomo—a group of folks in the same boat as I, to take counsel with. I had expected that group to be other parents of hemophiliacs. I knew all these people in my area; I knew that even if they weren't affected when Ryan was, they would be soon enough. However, these hemophiliac families felt terrified that I would identify them, and they were fiercely determined not to have anybody know who they were. So they shunned me. They were afraid of me. Which was really another way of saying they were afraid of Kokomo. An old friend of mine had a sister whose two sons were hemophiliacs. The sister left town rather than allow her boys to be victims of the same kind of discrimination and prejudice that had afflicted Ryan. I understood her flight, but I couldn't understand why she never called me, and I felt abandoned.

Years later, after Ryan died, she got in touch with me. Just out of the blue. She said she wanted me to know that she was really sorry she couldn't be there for me when Ryan was sick. "When the trouble began," said this woman. "I just had to keep quiet and not draw attention to my boys."

One of the reasons I always talked to the people who called me in the spring and summer of 1990 was that I knew how much help that unhappy woman and I could have been to each other in the spring and summer of 1985. It was a piece of me which had always been missing—the piece that involved an understanding community. As usual, it was provided by what I call "my public sector."

The first year after Ryan's death, Phil did an anniversary show to remember my boy. Then, on the fifth anniversary of Ryan's death, Phil did another anniversary show that featured forty kids, now young adults, who had been members of the audience in the first show Phil did with Ryan when he was alive.

Because of those shows, I met a number of other AIDS mothers and some of them affected me in important ways. I met John Keets and his mother, Liz; Douglas Gayton and his mother, Kathy; Jeremy Brooks and his mother, Kim; Zachary Strange and his mother, Vicky; Keith Crofoot and his mother, Deanna; Brett Lykins and his mother, Marty; Jason Robertson and his mother, Tammy.

I had known Tammy since the eighties. We met originally at the Elton John benefit for Athletes and Entertainers for Kids, and then did several fund-raising events together. We talked all the time on the phone. She had to move several times because community reaction was so bad.

Louise Ray had made contact some years before, when she saw us on television. She told me that she and her husband, Clifford, lived in Arcadia, Florida, and had three hemophiliac sons—Ricky,

Randy and Robbie—and one daughter, Candy. The family had been receiving death threats.

One night, past eleven-thirty, Louise called me and said, "Well, they did it."

"What?"

"They did it. They burned our house down."

I was shocked.

"We have nothing now," she said. "Nothing."

In subsequent years, Ryan and the Ray children did many benefits and media appearances together, and a recent bill to recompense hemophiliac families is named for Ricky, who has died. The Rays moved to Sarasota, where the school accepted them. I remember the occasion when the Sarasota school and Hamilton Heights High (as well as the children themselves) received awards from Surgeon General C. Everett Koop for leading the fight against AIDS. I think Dr. Koop is one of the greatest men of our century. I was so impressed with his charisma and his dignity. Like Dr. Myers, he fought for the truth no matter what. I think the fearless way in which he took on the cigarette industry and helped Americans unhook themselves from the smoking habit has saved thousands and thousands of lives. As for AIDS, the powers-that-be might not have wanted to listen to him, but Dr. Koop told it like it was anyway. He didn't buckle under pressure from anyone.

On the *Donahue* show in 1991, I also met Carol DiPaolo and her son, Joey, a down-to-earth, sincere kind of a kid, not a showboat, who had been born with a heart problem and had contracted AIDS from a transfusion when he was just a little baby. Carol and I became involved in a terrific organization called Mothers' Voices, which was started by New York women to make people aware of

AIDS. Carol and I have remained friends. Every time I go to New York, she invites me to her house for a big spaghetti dinner.

Another lasting relationship developed between me and Liz Keets, from Canton, Illinois. Her son, John, was a real tall boy, easygoing and thoughtful. He had von Willebrand's disease, a form of hemophilia, and developed full-blown AIDS in 1989. When his school learned he had AIDS, they did everything to help him and to keep his life as normal as possible. His hometown held several marches in his honor, to raise money for AIDS research. I was pleased to be among those invited to join in.

"I know I'm going to Heaven when I die," John once said. "So that doesn't scare me. It's just that I don't want to leave everyone . . . It really makes me hurt, knowing I may not get a chance at life. If I shed a tear for everything that hurts, I probably would evaporate."

One of the first things we did after establishing the Ryan White Foundation was to give out annual awards (now called Ryan's Angel Awards) to salute people who had been active in the fight against AIDS. And one of our first awards went to John Keets. He died in 1992.

In other moments in the public sector of my life, there were many people who had a great impact on me. One of them was Walter Dunn of Coca-Cola. I called him to thank him for all the help he and the company had given us over the years, and we got to talking. Walter told me he had just lost his wife to cancer. "I know what you're going through," he said. "It's really been so hard on me, too." And we just sat on the phone together for a bit, sharing our feelings about how you manage to live through the days, one by one.

When I did the *Geraldo* show, I met a woman named Sonia Singleton from Miami. Her drug-addict boyfriend had given her

AIDS. I just loved Sonia. She refused to be sad and down. She wore bright-colored clothes and kept a happy smile on her face. She died in February 1992. But I hold this image of her in my mind, that she fought the evil disease with good cheer and great faith, and that always inspired me.

Also on that show I met Dawn Wolf. She was infected and so was one of her sons. (Not the other. One of the most shocking features of AIDS is the randomness of its selection, the way it suddenly swerves and spares somebody who was standing right in its path . . . for no reason that anyone can yet understand.) Dawn has been tireless in going out with her children and speaking to groups of people to make them more aware of the danger of AIDS.

Many of the HIV children I met in those days are gone now. If I need to talk, there are—sadly—plenty of bereaved parents who know exactly what I've been through and with whom I can share my feelings. But it will always seem ironic to me that those who became my confidants were people I met on talk shows, or at public fund-raising events—and not people I met in my own hometown. Maybe it's for that reason that one of the most touching events that ever happened was that Ryan and I were voted Man and Woman of the Year by the readers of the *Indianapolis Star* in 1991. How Ryan would have loved knowing that among his own neighbors, he was finally considered a hero!

I have tried in my way to protect other people in my community from the same isolation that affected me when Ryan became ill. Every year since he died, in December around Christmastime, I have an open house for local people with AIDS and their families. It's nothing fancy, just a get-together with cake and homemade sugar cookies and punch, where folks can come and see all the decorations

I've been working on since September and enjoy themselves and feel like there's somebody out there who really cares about them.

Matt Frewer came to see us a few weeks after Ryan died. He asked me whether I had thought about what sort of monument I wanted to put up for my son. I hadn't thought anything about it. He said, "Well, whatever you decide you want, I'd like to take care of it." With this sensitive, generous gesture, Matt wanted to guarantee that I would not have to hesitate in creating the monument Ryan deserved.

I thought very hard about the needs of strangers when planning that monument. In all the mail we received, it seemed as though folks wanted a piece of Ryan, almost as though his memory gave them strength. I saw how other kids admired Ryan. They felt like they were blessed if they had known him. I wanted the stone to be a way of meeting him for all those who had never had the chance to do that when he was alive. For the rest of us in the AIDS community, I wanted the monument to serve history. A hundred years down the road, when this nightmare is just an old story, I wanted people to be able to look at the monument and remember.

It took me weeks of planning to make sure that the stone was just perfect.

I sat down with my friend Mary Baker and began to try and imagine what might be written on Ryan's stone. I felt it should tell Ryan's story and honor his cause. So I told the man at Waverly Monuments that I wanted it real tall, because Ryan had always wanted to be tall and had greatly admired men like Howie and Kareem Abdul-Jabbar, who were both way over six feet. The monument maker had a big piece of stone, six feet eight inches high, in tones of gray and white and black. When Mary and I saw it, we thought: *Yes! This is what Ryan would have wanted.*

On the base, we had the words that Bill Shaw of *People* magazine had ascribed to Ryan: Patience, Tolerance, Faith, Love, Forgiveness, Wisdom, Spirit. On the front, our stone carver created a cross with Ryan's picture in the center, and above it a bird flying away, like the skyline pigeon in Elton's song. I wanted the words to Elton's "Candle in the Wind" and the words to Michael's "Man in the Mirror," the words about making a difference, making it right. That was one of Ryan's favorite songs. When Michael came to our house after the funeral, he and Andrea sat down in the red Mustang. Michael turned the key. "Man in the Mirror" came on over the tape. Ryan would play that song over and over again because the words were so meaningful to him. It was the last song Ryan had listened to in that car.

We put the words of Reverend Bud Probasco from the funeral service on the stone, and the words that Dr. Kleiman said right after Ryan died, to the effect that he had passed away without pain. It seemed to be terribly important to many people to be reassured of that. We also added Governor Evan Bayh's comment that Ryan would be remembered more for what he taught us about living than for the disease that afflicted him.

When I told the monument man I wanted a cartoon on the stone, too, he looked at me as though I was crazy. It seemed such a tacky idea in the midst of all these inspirational messages. He didn't realize I meant Jim Borgman's Pulitzer Prize-winning cartoon of Ryan being hugged by St. Peter in "a place where no one is afraid to hug." It summed up in one moving image Ryan's struggle and his victory.

Finally, I thought, since all these kids were always asking for

Ryan's autograph, I would have his signature carved on the stone so that they could visit the grave and bring paper and rub over it and take a piece of Ryan back home with them.

That gravestone has been a magnet for young people. They leave gifts and notes—a teddy bear, a candy cane at Christmas. On his nineteenth birthday, we found a bottle of Budweiser on the grave with a note that said, "This Bud's for you, Ryan." A girl named Shannon came from Chicago with her boyfriend last year and cleaned up the whole gravesite of all winter's debris. She told me she had made the trip for the past five years. The sweetness of that pilgrimage just overwhelms me.

Then sometimes something happens which makes you realize that the anger and hatred we've tried so hard to forget still festers in a few hearts. I was watering the flowers on Ryan's grave this past spring, and a big red truck pulled out of a lot nearby. The driver leaned out of the cab and yelled to me: "Bitch!" Like I was his enemy. Like that boy in the ground and his mom watering the flowers on his grave had done that driver and his big truck an evil turn.

Will Kokomo, Indiana, never get over the Whites? Will this hatred go on forever?

Back when Ryan had died, I met a woman at the cemetery named Bucky Poppleton. She had lost her teenage daughter because the girl had an epileptic seizure at the lake and drowned.

Bucky's daughter's grave is down from Ryan's. There is no stone, but there are many decorations. At Christmastime, she puts a big manger scene there. One year, somebody stole the baby Jesus out of it—and I just remember thinking: *Who would have done such an awful thing?*

Bucky passed by Ryan's grave one day and saw that somebody had toppled Ryan's stone. She reported it to the police.

One of the boys who knocked over the headstone was brought to me by his minister, to ask my forgiveness. Of course I forgave him. But while he was there in my house, I asked him, "Why? Why would you go in the dead of night and turn over a stone that was marked with words like 'Patience, tolerance, faith, love, forgiveness, wisdom and spirit'? Why?"

This child said, "I didn't like the attention Ryan got because he had AIDS."

It was unbelievable! He was jealous of Ryan! As though Ryan would not have given all the world to *not* have had that attention.

"Would you like to change places with him?" I asked this boy. "No," he said.

His minister wanted me to drop the charges. I refused. They were not criminal charges; I knew this boy would not undergo any serious punishment for his deed. But I wanted him and his parents to have to pay to repair that stone, to understand how jealousy had twisted and distorted their way of thinking.

They weren't the only folks who had conceived a jealousy towards us. Strange as it may seem, some people actually thought of us as "lucky" because we had met all kinds of celebrities and gone to all kinds of glitzy events. They envied us our "good fortune."

They called me and demanded that I get Michael Jackson to invite them to his ranch and Phil Donahue to put them on his show and Elton John to fly them to his concerts. If ever I could arrange something for these folks, I did. I remember a caring school nurse who called on behalf of a boy who was suffering from AIDS and whose family had virtually abandoned him. In this hideous situation, she was reaching for something, anything that could brighten this boy's last months. I called the Make-A-Wish Foundation, which does such fine work in providing sick kids with their hearts' desires.

They found someone to give the boy a computer, because he wanted to record his thoughts and feelings at the end. I remember asking Michael Jackson's office to send a memento to a kid named Rocky who was Michael's biggest fan. Like Elton's office, they were immediately generous in cases like that.

But what could you say to a woman who demanded that Michael buy her a Cadillac? How could you react to the woman who called up Elton's office and pretended to be me and said Ryan wanted concert tickets?

My son had written a book. Folks called, wanting me to arrange things so their children, too, could write books that would become best-sellers. And if I did not have the power to make that happen, then they were consumed with envy and lashed out in anger.

Recently a lady came up to me after a speech and told me this story. Her eight-year-old daughter, she said, had died of cancer, and she had always been very bitter about all the money that was going to AIDS when she felt like cancer should get much more. "I always resented you," she said, "because of all the publicity you brought to AIDS. And when I came to hear you speak, I realized that you were a mom who had lost her child, just like me."

We're all hurting; we're all in such pain. None of us wanted to lose our child. It doesn't matter what the cause of the tragedy— whether it's AIDS or cancer or a drunk driver—not one of us is luckier than another, because there is no good luck in this situation. We are all the same in our loss and our grief.

In the early summer of 1991, I made the fateful decision to quit Delco, take the buyout they were offering and go to work as head of the newly formed Ryan White Foundation.

We set up a whole program of AIDS information for young people. We hired workers who were especially trained to talk to the hundreds of folks who call. I signed up with the Keppler agency.

At first they wanted me to write out my speech—prepare the jokes, set it all in stone. Mr. Keppler sent me some samples—in particular, a great speech by Suzanne Somers. I tried to write a speech like hers, but it just wasn't me and I felt I would never be able to make it work.

Much of the time when you go on a speaking tour—for example, the eleven-city tour I took to promote *Ryan White: My Own Story*, which Ann Marie Cunningham and Ryan had written—your hosts will say that they want you here and here and here. And then when you get to town, they suddenly add, "And here and here and these three radios stations and these two TV stations, and this little press conference before, and this little luncheon after; it's easy, it's on the way . . ." If I had been Elizabeth Taylor, nobody would ever have even dared to try taking advantage of me this way. But I was Jeanne White, the famous pushover, so they pushed. And Shelley, bless her, learned to politely, pleasantly, push back. If it had been entirely up to me, I probably would have booked myself every night and never come home. Shelley protected me from my own inability to say no. She arranged everything for me when I traveled and defended me against broken promises.

When I had to go out and speak, Shelley would come with me (Phil's orders; he didn't want me traveling by myself). She was my biggest fan and my best critic. She'd always tell me what she thought of my speeches, what to keep in, what to eliminate. Although we had started out just as co-workers, these trips drew Shelley and me into a close friendship, and that made the trips themselves a lot more fun for both of us. We'd talk until all hours of the night. We'd always stop in a miniature store to find an item for my dollhouse. I also started shopping in the nice new stores for big women to get myself some pretty clothes (Andrea's orders; she wanted her mom to look spiffy).

Making speeches made me a nervous wreck. All day long, I would fret about the speech. I would try to arrive at the site of my appearance real early in the morning, even though the speech was at night. I couldn't eat because I was afraid I would have to go to the bathroom in the middle of the speech. I would say it out loud. I would end up not saying what I had been working on. Trying to stick to a prepared speech was getting me all messed up. I thought: *The only thing I can do is just tell my story. If I tell my own story, then I won't get messed up and I won't have to worry. I know my story better than anybody.*

It took me about eight or nine months to get to that point; probably close to two years before I became really comfortable. The pattern was usually very similar from one place to another. I would have to put people in the picture by starting over with a video—generally I used the segment of CBS's "West 57th Street" produced by Jude Dratt—to remind everybody of what Ryan had gone through. Then I would talk about what had happened to us and why it was so important for parents and children to protect each other against AIDS, why it was so important for the government to help people suffering with AIDS, how frank we had to be about sex and sexually transmitted diseases, even if that offended our sensibilities. Then there would be questions.

Since I didn't write the speech, I never said exactly the same thing. And since every audience was different, the questions were never quite the same. But by and large, people had one desire—to hear about Ryan White, to hear about the demands on the caregiver, to know what they could do to save themselves and those they loved.

Before each address, I'd go off by myself and say a prayer. "Dear Lord, please help me do my very best and educate everybody—Ryan, please be by my side and help me, too." I would say it repeatedly, over and over, like a chant, and wait for this feeling to rise up inside me, a kind of psychic security blanket. And then, when the spirit and the purpose had filled me up, I would go out there and make my speech.

As long as I have the prayer and the feeling, I'm okay. It comes from Ryan, I know. It is all that I need.

One of the most delightful events I attended during that period was a fund-raising fair for the Wisconsin Hemophilia Association in March of 1991. It was an important occasion for me, because I had been such a pariah in the hemophilia community in the mid-eighties. Before the speech and the dinner, they had a little fair to raise some money. It centered on fortune-telling (something which I had never approved of, since it seemed so pagan and un-Christian). However, this fair was a real hoot. The place was full of colorful swamis and palm readers and numerologists. For five dollars, you could have a grand old time.

This palm reader looked at my hand and said that the last broken piece of Jeanne White was about to be repaired, that I was going to meet a man.

Well, that was such an outlandish idea that it just about knocked me off my chair. "Oh, boy, that's all I need!" I laughed. "A man in my life!"

Exactly one year later, I fell in love.

Chapter 7

"Don't ask me until I know I can say yes."

I was so tossed and prodded and pushed after Ryan's death that I all but lost contact with some of my closest neighbors. The Ginder family, for example, whose father had been so kind to Ryan, just sort of slipped out of my consciousness.

The last I remembered seeing Roy Ginder was sometime shortly before Ryan's death, when we were about to take our last trip to California. After we returned, Ryan was so sick and I had so much to worry about that it never occurred to me to get in touch with this man who had shared my son's obsession with his car.

It turned out that he and his family had gone to Florida during spring break, and his wife liked it so well there that they decided to relocate. They heard on the news that Ryan was very ill, and Roy brought the family back to Indiana a couple of days early, because he hoped to see Ryan once more before he died. But it was too late. Ryan was already gone.

Ryan's death saddened and surprised Roy. He was one of those people who was more affected by Ryan's liveliness and determination than by the medical details of his condition. While they were sitting in the body shop, talking about rims and tires, planning how Ryan would one day work as his apprentice, Roy just couldn't quite believe that Ryan was terminally ill.

He took his children to the viewing at the funeral home. They tried to attend Ryan's funeral, too, and stood for a long time on line in the rain. I don't remember seeing them. To be honest, I recall very little of who was there and who wasn't. The trauma of a loss makes you blind and deaf and dumb. Your face is saying, "Thank you for coming; how nice of you to come; yes, he was a wonderful boy; thank you; yes; thank you . . ." but your mind is far away, in a cloud of memories.

I chanced to meet Roy during this difficult time because Andrea and I were thinking of giving Ryan's Mustang to the Children's Museum in Indianapolis—and no sooner had we made that decision than somebody backed into the beautiful car and messed it all up. All that careful, artistic work, scratched and dented—it was a real shame.

I went over to the body shop with my mom and asked Roy if he could repair the damage. He was a big, thick, strong man with light brown hair and pale blue eyes. His uniform was covered with grease and grime; his face and hands were smeared. When he said yes, I knew I could trust that the Mustang would soon be as good as new.

I do remember looking back in through the body-shop door as we left, and thinking: *Well, now, that is really a cute guy.*

As soon as I thought that thought, I was just dumbstruck with guilt. *A married man, Jeanne! What has happened to you?! Have you gone nuts?!* Immediately, I explained to myself that the reason I had entertained this passing thought about Roy Ginder was that Ryan had spoken so well of him and that now that I had talked with him myself, I saw that he was a real down-to-earth guy and that every-thing nice Ryan had said about him was true. And I just remember dropping it at that. I never thought about Roy again after he fixed the car.

The Ginders sold their house and in August they moved. Roy's best friend lived in Florida and wasn't very optimistic about the prospects of finding a job there. It was 1990. The economy had slowed down. But there's something about Roy that makes people trust him. He did his version of what Hollywood calls networking. The first day he was there, he went fishing with his friend and the local Baptist preacher. The second day he was there, he attended services at the preacher's church. The third day he had an interview with the manager of a big body shop. The fourth day, he had a job. Three, maybe four people had met Roy Ginder, and that was all it took for him to be accepted into the community.

The move to Florida was not to last long. No sooner had the whole family settled into their new life than Mrs. Ginder decided she really wanted to come home. Roy had to stay behind, because he couldn't just walk out on these folks who had been so trusting of him and had given him such a good job. He had to give notice, allow some time for his boss to replace him (which wasn't going to be easy).

Since the house had been sold, Mrs. Ginder stayed with her

mother until she could find an apartment. Roy came home after a few weeks, in time for Thanksgiving. He and his wife split about nine months later. She moved out. He stayed with the kids. Eventually he became a foreman at a construction company.

It was real tough for him to be a single father. Roy was one of those guys who never knew how to do stuff in the house. He could rehabilitate cars, lay brick, fix anything in the world, he was quite the handyman, but ask him to make dinner and he went into a panic and headed for McDonald's. His children weren't babies, they were all in their teens, but their mom had always done all the housework, so they didn't know how to do much at home either. According to folks who knew them, the Ginder household was pretty hectic after the mom departed.

Roy speaks of his marriage now as though the breakup didn't hurt him, like he expected it and handled it real calmly.

Personally, I believe that a lot of his apparent calm was just not wanting to admit how badly he had been hurt, always having to appear to be this big, strong, skilled man who could take whatever life had to give him and remain in control of his emotions. I think the real truth is that it must have been an awfully miserable time for him.

One night while Roy was still in Florida, I was sitting in Ryan's room. Just sitting there on the bed, remembering. Suddenly the phone rang. It was Roy Ginder.

"Jeanne. Hi."

"Hi."

"Just calling to see how you were doing—I still had Ryan's number . . ."

"I'm fine."

"Well, that's good."

166

"How about you, Roy?"

"I'm fine."

There was a silence. The weight of that most common of ordinary, everyday lies—"I'm fine"—lay heavy on the conversation.

"You know, we moved," he said.

"Oh, yeah?"

He gave me his new address.

"If they ever have that benefit in Ryan's honor, be sure and let me know. I'd like to bring the kids."

"Okay."

"So you take care now, Jeanne."

"You, too, Roy."

"Bye."

"Bye."

I was so involved in my own grief then that it never occurred to me that the man on the phone was suffering too; that he was reaching out to me in some way that wasn't yet defined for either of us.

I couldn't imagine that there was anybody in the world at that moment who felt as lonely and forsaken as I.

I sent him a Christmas card.

It wasn't a personal thing. Shelley was doing up a whole list of people to send cards to for Christmas from me and the newly forming Ryan White Foundation. We sent out hundreds of cards that year. I didn't think anything about it. But Roy did. When his daughter, Shawn, showed him that card, he felt a little bit encouraged. He asked her, "Do you think Mrs. White is going out with anybody?" Shawn, then a sophomore, said she would ask Andrea, then a senior, at school, but it kind of slipped her mind and she didn't remember to ask until she happened to bump into Andrea in the hall one day a few weeks later.

Andrea came home and said, "Mom, do you remember Roy Ginder?"

"Yes."

"Did you know he got a divorce?"

"Yes, I did hear that."

"Would you go out with him?"

"Well, I don't know."

"Well, his daughter, Shawn, says he wanted to know if you're dating anybody and if you're not, would you go out with him?"

"Well . . ."

"Go for it, Mom."

Andrea turned and left me there in my kitchen. She had never known me to go on a date; I don't think she really thought I would do it. But I do knew she was just tickled to death at my confusion, and enjoying her role as message-carrier.

It took about three months from the time I sent the Christmas card for all these messages to get delivered. By that time, Roy's mother and grandmother had moved in with him, and he had things at home a little bit more under control. And I suppose he would have gotten around to calling me one day—but as fate would have it, I ended up calling him first.

Karen Engledow, the first executive director of the Ryan White Foundation, had asked her friend Paul Rosenfeld, a successful event coordinator, to make available her beautiful apartment for a cocktail party to which Karen had invited some very prominent Indianapolis people. The purpose of the party was not just social. Karen and Paula wanted to interest these folks in the new foundation. Earl Nightingale, manager of the Hyatt Regency in downtown Indianapolis, was there. He would eventually become president of our board. Dennis Stover was there. He is also a board member, now in Washington, D.C., working with the National AIDS Fund there.

Even though Shelley and her husband, Tom, were going with me, and would see to it I got there and back home all right, I still didn't want to be a third wheel. I so didn't want to have to go alone—again. Shelley suggested that since Roy had already expressed an interest in me, I might not be going way out on a limb if I called and asked him to come with me.

"What do you think, Andrea?"

"Go for it, Mom."

So I called Roy Ginder.

He said sure, he'd be happy to come. He sounded real relaxed about it and asked me what he should wear. I said, "Oh, you can just go casual."

Little did I know that these words struck terror into the heart of this big, strong man. The minute we hung up the phone, he went into a total panic and called his buddy, who worked with him at the construction company, who was single and in Roy's estimation a sophisticated expert on the dating scene.

"Billy! Help! I've got this date with this woman. She says it's a cocktail party and I should dress casual. What does 'casual' mean to you?"

"A sweater. Maybe a turtleneck. Slacks."

"Oh, Lord, what am I gonna do? All I've got is my body-shop uniforms and my Levi's and a couple of sweatshirts and a Sunday shirt for church!"

Roy's sophisticated friend immediately concluded that they had to go shopping for clothes at Wal-Mart on Route 31 in Carmel. They bought slacks and a sweater and even shoes, because the only shoes Roy had that weren't work boots were his ten-year-old penny loafers.

Paula Rosenfeld's condo, like Paula herself, was elegant and classy, in an upscale Indy neighborhood. It had a white carpet and a white baby grand piano. Roy says he had to control an impulse to take off his shoes when we walked in. He watched the guests walking around, eating and drinking and not spilling anything on that carpet, and he figured he'd better stay away from the refreshments. I could see that these were unfamiliar surroundings for him, and he was really shy and kind of embarrassed. Shelley's husband is the same kind of guy as Roy—likes his basketball game and his fries and a good joke—and him being there put Roy somewhat at ease. But after a while, Tom and Shelley drifted off and I saw that Roy was standing alone, not knowing whom to talk to, feeling like everybody was staring at him. So even though I had a lot of socializing to do myself, and a lot of folks to meet and greet and talk to about AIDS education, I kept going back to him, to make sure he knew that I hadn't forgotten him and that I was pleased he was my date.

Little by little, people began talking to Roy. I could see him smiling, his face relaxed and interested. After the party, Shelley and Tom and Roy and I went out to the Waffle House for a bite. And it came up that one of the men Roy had been talking to was gay. Well, Roy could hardly believe that. He said he didn't know whether he could ever approve of anybody who was gay and didn't understand how Christian mothers like me and Shelley could be involved with the gay community.

This little dark needle of doubt now entered what had been a great evening. How could I imagine that a devout Seventh-Day Adventist like Roy Ginder could ever get over his suspicion of homosexuals and accept me and my work and my friends?

At the end of the evening, he took me up to the door and just said good night. Not a handshake; nothing.

I thought: *Too bad, Jeanne. He had a rotten time and felt intimidated and he doesn't agree with your politics and you'll never hear from him again.*

Then he said, "I really enjoyed myself tonight. Your friends are very interesting. I'd like to see you again."

I thought: *Yesss!* and went inside the house and sagged back against my front door and breathed a sigh of relief for having successfully endured my first date in years.

Two or three days later, Roy called. He came over to my house limping and in pain. He had injured his knee at work and now it was throbbing something awful. I remember he hauled his leg up on the coffee table, hoping that if he kept it elevated, some of the swelling would go down and the pain diminish. It turned out I knew just what to do for that knee. When Ryan would have a bleed in his knee, there would be no place for the blood to go, and the joint area would swell and become terribly painful. Through the years I had learned how to rub the knee with the tips of my fingers, just hard enough to give some relief, not so hard as to cause discomfort. I would rub for hours sometimes, so that my hand would ache from the repetitive motion. But it would make Ryan feel better, and he'd relax and sometimes he would be able to go to sleep. So when Roy Ginder came over with this swelled-up leg and that grim line of pain set in his jaw, I just rubbed my fingertips over the hurting part like I had done for Ryan. Roy closed his eyes and leaned back.

"Gosh, that feels so good. I've never known anybody who would do something like that for me," he said. He smiled at me, a very gentle smile. "Thank you, Jeanne. Thank you."

*   *   *

I thought maybe he still had feelings for his ex-wife. So the next day, when I saw my neighbor Karen, who was Mrs. Ginder's friend, step outside to get mail, I struck up a conversation. She was real friendly and talkative, and she told me that she'd heard Roy was dating somebody.

I thought: *Won't she be surprised to find out it's me!*

Then she said she had heard it was this woman from Roy's church who was a devout Seventh-Day Adventist. My neighbor had heard they were thinking of getting married.

That conversation on my neighbor's lawn gave me a major case of the miseries. I knew that Roy had been going to church real regular since his wife had left. He was making the kids go with him and using the church as a moral support, assuring himself that they were being raised in a Christian way, even though he had to work and leave them on their own so much.

I thought: *For sure, a woman he knows from church is going to have a better chance of getting close to him than I do.*

When next I saw Roy, I came right out and asked him about her. He told me that she was just somebody who liked to send her boys to hockey games with him and his boys, and that they were just parenting buddies.

On our next date we went to the movies—with Roy's sons, Adam and Steve, sitting right behind us. I remember it—*Fried Green Tomatoes*—but I don't think I watched much of it. I was too busy worrying: *Why doesn't he hold my hand?! Why doesn't he try to kiss me?! Something's wrong! Maybe he really doesn't like me.* Then I remembered what Ryan had said: "Mr. Ginder is a super guy, Mom." So I grabbed Roy's hand and leaned over and gave him a little kiss on the neck. I couldn't believe I did that. But it was reassuring that Steve and Adam gave me a big smile.

Afterwards we went back to my house.

"What is the matter with you, Roy Ginder? I can't believe I had to kiss you first."

"Well, it wasn't 'cause I didn't want to. I was just kind of nervous. I didn't want you to think I was being too forward."

"Oh, for Heaven's sake . . ."

And he put his big arms around me and all the childish tension between us just melted away and that was that.

What appealed to me so much about Roy Ginder was his honesty, his down-to-earth attitude and his trusting nature. I couldn't ever understand how his ex-wife had let him go.

He wasn't just looking for some woman to take up the slack. He was looking for a family-maker. And because he had known Ryan so well and, through him, our family, it turned out that he looked my way.

As those wonderful weeks went by, I found that I was so crazy about Roy, so thrilled to hear his soft, drawling, tenor voice on the phone, so excited to hear the sound of his old truck in my driveway, that I began to get scared.

"This is moving too fast," I said to Shelley. "I'm too nuts for him. It's frightening."

My whole life had been my son's illness. I hadn't had a date in years and years; sex had become a distant memory. Now all of a sudden I was involved in a love affair. Could it possibly be that in a matter of weeks, this easygoing man could change all my plans and shift all my priorities?

I liked his values; I liked his morals; I thought he was incredibly attractive. I have to admit I liked him because Ryan had liked him so much, because Ryan had been such a good judge of character and because they'd shared something so special. But for many years I had been going to parties with kindhearted gay men, safe in the knowledge that they were wonderful friends and never potential lovers. "Maybe I've been desperate for love for so long that now I'm just in love with the idea of being in love!" I said to Shelley.

Andrea came home from school, all upset. She had heard from Shawn, Roy's daughter, that he was thinking about asking me to marry him, that he had discussed it with his kids to see if they would like to have me as their stepmom. And the kids had said yes.

Andrea expressed some serious doubts about the whole thing. She already had a warmhearted, loving stepfather in Steve Ford; she didn't feel like she needed another one. Even though she liked Roy, she thought our courtship was going way too fast. And I think she was really annoyed that Roy's daughter had told her about this, that somehow his kids "knew" more than she did.

I told Andrea there was nothing to know yet, that she was my friend and my confidante and my partner in everything, and I would never take one step without telling her first. But now I was kind of pre-warned. When Roy called me that night and said he had something really important he wanted to ask me, I said, "Don't ask me until I know I can say yes."

I was worried. My own daughter, a level-headed, independent-minded girl, was not happy with these developments. She would never have stood in my way, but she sure wanted to make absolutely certain I didn't do anything stupid. My best friends—Shelley Henson, Mary Baker, Betsy Stewart—said to take it easy. They all liked Roy. It was the children they worried about. Adam was thirteen, Steve was fourteen, Shawn was sixteen and Andrea was going on eighteen—hard years to accept stepparents.

Hesitations and suspicions began to kick in again as my relation-

ship with Roy got better and better. The thing about being alone
is that it has certain advantages, especially for women, and one of
them is personal freedom. As a working mom who had been taking
care of others all her life, I had grown to treasure my freedom, and
I was nervous about giving it up.

When Ryan was ill, I had felt like I had too many other things
to worry about, that my focus had to be on my two children, that
I had no time for a man. Since I had started earning a good living
as a speaker and educator, I had enjoyed the freedom to spend my
money the way I wanted, without anybody else telling me different.
For the first time in my life, I could buy what I liked; I didn't have
to settle for something that somebody else had to approve of, too.
I loved that I could just decorate a house to suit my tastes alone. I
didn't want to have to ask some man what he thought.

I was also worried about finances and the future, as every woman
who's considering marriage ought to be. I felt like everything we
had was because of Ryan. We had a really nice house now. I was
afraid of making a deal in which Andrea would lose the house after
I was gone. I didn't want to share everything again and then lose
everything again. Phil had once done a show where kids came on
who reported that their folks had remarried and everything they had
went to the new parents. I swore that would never happen to my
Andrea. It was we three who'd had to battle the world with Ryan's
illness; just us three, nobody else. If Andrea wanted to sell the house
after I was gone, that was her business; but I needed to feel secure
in the knowledge that she would have what was rightfully hers.

Roy and I talked about it. He understood exactly how I felt, and
we made our arrangements accordingly.

In order to acquaint Roy more fully with my life, I asked him
if he would come to Washington with me to lobby on the Ryan

White CARE Act. The Appropriations Committee had authorized the money for it, but had never come up with all the funding—and we were trying to make that happen so that all the AIDS programs could get going.

Because I'm in these situations all the time, working with government officials, I wanted to see how Roy reacted when faced with being around political people. I really admired the way he acted. We went to a party in one of those beautiful, narrow Georgetown houses with lovely antiques and lots of history. We met many people I had worked with over the years; I was real proud to show off Roy to them. These were people who knew my struggles. They were positive about my work. They had respect for me. One of the lawyers there got into a discussion with Roy about antique cars; another filled him in on the political background of the Ryan White CARE Act. It was a wonderful evening.

We walked outside into the calm evening. I took Roy's arm.

"Boy," he said, "this was really moving. Just to think this was about a bill named for Ryan in Washington, D.C. It's just now dawning on me how big and important all this is. I guess being the neighbor down the street, it was always impossible to believe. But now I know. You have got the best friends in the whole world." He kissed me and hugged me. I knew he was real proud.

"Roy, did you know that lawyer you were talking to was gay?"

"You've got to be kidding."

"And that other guy, the one who collects cars . . . Actually, honey, most of the people you met at the party tonight were gay."

"Say it ain't so!" He laughed. People who've been brought up the way Roy was, and the way I was, too, in homes where homosexuals are feared and scorned, have this feeling they can always tell who is gay. It inevitably comes as a big shock to discover that you don't know what you thought you knew for sure.

The next evening, we went to another dinner party with lots of politicians and their wives. Roy was examining everybody, trying to detect some trace of their sexual orientation. When we left he said, "Okay, now you're going to tell me that the old guy was gay and the blond guy was gay . . ."

"No, honey," I said. "The people who gave the party, they're a gay couple, but most of the guests were straight as you and me."

The political danger signal I had detected on our first date had to be talked through. To Roy, my association with what he thought of as liberal politics and my easy relationships in the gay community just didn't mix with the rest of me. As far as he was concerned, I was a conservative who happened to vote like a liberal. I seemed like just the sort of "old-fashioned girl" he had not been married to the first time around, whom he wanted very badly now. My weight didn't make any difference to him. (He's not a lightweight himself.) He wanted a companion he could trust, who would be loyal and supportive and always on his side. That was exactly what I wanted.

But my politics made me unsuitable in the eyes of many of his friends. Some of his church associates were just horrified that I had introduced Roy to people they considered to be wicked sinners.

"Listen, honey," I said, "I can't make a choice between you and people who I've been friends with for years and years who stood by me and helped me when nobody else would. I cannot all of a sudden say to these people: 'I'm marrying this homophobe, so I can't see you anymore.' That would be impossible, Roy. It would be wrong.

"This is me. This is my life. Love me. Love my friends."

The moment when I introduced Roy Ginder to my gay friends

in Washington, when they reached out and shook his hand, the warmth of their reception, the sincerity of their joy for us, that was the moment of no return for Roy Ginder.

Roy started looking at the gay community a lot differently after that trip. Today, he's even "hugging buddies" with a lot of my friends who are gay. That's something for Roy, to be able to hug a gay man and not be afraid everybody will think he's gay, too.

As our relationship grew definite, and folks in Cicero began to know we were determined to marry, Roy's ex-wife called him at work and said she needed to see him about the kids. She apparently was thinking that she wanted him back. There were all kinds of stories about them swirling around, possibly instigated by Roy's children. I had thought I would be able to trust Roy, that things would always be on the up-and-up with him. But now there was all this confusion around our relationship, and I didn't ever want to be in confusion again about a man.

I called him and told him to come over, and when he was standing in front of my face, I said I wanted us to break up for a while.

There was a long silence. He has a way of sighing, Roy does, like all the patience in the world is going to be required to get him through the next minute of his life.

"Now listen, Jeanne, you've got to believe me on this. I am not interested in my ex-wife. If the kids are talking about her and me getting back together, that's because they want us to, and they want us to because they are kids and kids always want their moms and dads to get back together. I do not want to go back to her. I do not want her in my life anymore. I want only you."

So that was it. Roy asked me to marry him—and I said yes.

In June of 1992, two months before our wedding, he and his children moved in with me and Andrea. It was vital to see if I could stand being a stepmom, if they could stand to live under my discipline. But living together was a controversial move. Roy had religious pressures to overcome. He thought if we were going to move in together, we should get separate rooms.

I said to him what my wise son, Ryan, had once said to me: 'It's about time we stopped worrying what other people think."

It turned out better—and worse—than I could ever have imagined. Roy and I were ecstatically happy together. Just to look at his face across my morning coffee was enough to bring me a sense of peace and well-being that I hadn't felt ever in my entire adult life.

We found that we were both, in our own ways, equally creative people, which meant we had a basic understanding that went to the very core of our personalities. Roy took over the garage, moved in his old cars and his welding and sanding equipment and all his cans of paint and grease and his tools, and left the rest of the house to me. "You do a fabulous job making this place look great, honey," he said to me, "and you should go on doing just that." I didn't mess with his garage; he didn't mess with my Christmas villages and my dollhouses and my beautiful garden. He had redone Ryan's car; then he redid the '57 Chevy that he later gave to his son Steven. Then he completely redid a '73 Corvette for us. Now he's doing a '32 Ford pickup truck. That was his life, his outlet, his therapy—and I understood it because I had mine, too.

We both turned out to be homebodies. I travel a lot for the Ryan White Foundation; I'm on the road for weeks out of the year— but nothing pleases me more than to come home again, to get settled next to Roy in front of the Indiana Pacers or the Colts game on Sunday afternoon and just be quiet and be home and be together.

My big mistake was in thinking I could be the superwoman of

stepmothers and change Roy's children. I was sure they would love my orderly, pretty, peaceful house so much that they'd just turn themselves over to me and let me transform them into disciplined, purposeful people who made good grades in school and learned a trade like their father. But it didn't work. I just couldn't change kids who were already in their teens when I met them, who had already been formed by the pressures of their lives. They had their own ideas of how life should be lived; they had their own mother and they loved her and no other woman was going to replace her, as much as Roy might have wanted that.

The kids enjoyed some of the things we had that Ryan had worked so hard and suffered so much to give us—the comfortable home, the trip to visit Michael Jackson at his ranch. But they resented the fact that my life and work were dedicated to making sure that Ryan would not have died and suffered in vain. I tried to explain to them that everything we had was because of what Ryan had done and the courageous way he had led his short life—but it wasn't easy for them to understand.

Our contacts with the world of the famous threw Roy's kids in a lot of ways. And I had my sensitivities, too. I couldn't stand it when the kids pretended to be sick in order to stay home from school.

"My boy was really sick!" I cried. "He was nauseous, throwing up. He lost his hair, he ran fevers . . . and he would have done anything to go to school! Every morning he crawled out of bed and got into his shower and dressed and begged the world to let him go to school, and you're standing here with a report card full of bad grades, telling me you've got a headache and you can't go!"

It was never going to work between us.

Our lives had just been too different.

Shawn went to live with her mom, then married and had a baby.

Adam has moved back and forth between his mom's house and our house. The middle child—Steven—has stayed on with us. I have had to accept his ways, and he has had to accept mine. The biggest part of stepparenting is sometimes accepting what you *cannot* do, and then going on from there.

I wonder sometimes if the photos and memorabilia about Ryan in my house upset Roy's kids. I even wonder if they upset my Andrea. Do these children feel they have to compete with a ghost for my affections? Are they sensitive to or intimidated by Ryan's fame, like the boy who threw over his gravestone? It occasionally occurs to me that maybe I should clear the walls of his image, toss out his old stuff.

But every time I think that, every time I am tempted to toss out the dead to salve the feelings of the living, I think no, that would only kill him more and kill me a little and solve nothing.

It is not unhealthy to keep your memories alive. When you let your memories die, you take that away from who you are. *Sure, it's bad to be obsessed. If I were to go into Ryan's room and cry my eyes out all the time, that would be a mistake. But that is not what happens. The memories come and they comfort you and they keep your child with you.*

When I'm in the house—which was the house Ryan got for us—and I remember him, I laugh as much as I cry. I feel like his spirit is with me. I like to keep his room the way he had it, with all the cars and action figures and posters and mementos. I remember how he'd like to have his jeans folded just a certain way and nobody could fold those jeans but him. Sometimes when Andrea and I look at a pair of jeans coming out of the dryer, we'll think about that, the two of us at the same time, and have a laugh. To include your loved ones in your life is really good—provided you include the good times and the laughter and not just the sad times at the end.

Back in the days before Ryan took sick. I had a girlfriend named Susan who made Andrea's skating outfits and who had lost her little girl in a train wreck. She had this portrait of her daughter in her house. I thought: Boy, it must be hard to have to look at that all the time. But when it happened to me, I realized it wasn't hard at all. That little girl was the pride of Susan's life, just like Ryan was the pride of my life. To keep the child close, to keep the picture always there, that was a real comfort.

I have a big problem with erasing somebody from your life. When my mom and dad go, I'm not going to throw out everything of theirs and erase them. Dead or alive, your family is your family.

Roy and I were married on August 1, 1992.

More than two hundred people came. Family. Old friends and new. For two months, I had been taking the stones off Andrea's skating outfits—pearls and sequins and aurora beads—and sewing them on my wedding dress.

We held up the wedding because the car that was bringing Phil and Marlo got lost and made them late. They ended up having to get dressed in a truck stop. The clock ticked; the guests squirmed; my ravishing maid of honor Andrea gave me that "time to get started, Mom" look. However, I felt like I just couldn't get married until Phil and Marlo walked through that door. They were the people who had, in the wake of Ryan's death, helped me start over.

Phil had introduced me to abilities I never knew I had. He kept persuading me that I could have a new career as a speaker and a teacher. He stayed involved, helped me build the Ryan White Foundation. If ever I felt like I couldn't do it, Phil kept me going. He had shaped the future for me.

My wedding to Roy Ginder meant that the future was here.

Chapter 8

Lessons Learned in Rooms Full of Strangers

Now that I travel around the country, making speeches to promote AIDS education, people say to me: "Oh, you have such a glamorous life, getting to go here and there, visiting so many places." But they don't see the other side, how lonely it is living in hotel rooms, how much I miss my family when I'm away.

You go and pour your heart out to a room full of strangers; you pour your strength into them to help them, to save them; you hear what they have to say back to you and you try to take all the lessons to heart. And then you go back to your hotel room and you're all alone.

Now, how glamorous is that?

My travels have taught me a great deal about the fears and desires of my country. But mostly they have taught me a great deal about myself.

I always felt like we all had choices, that every one of us could make our own opportunities in life. Then I went traveling, and I met people who had no choices, not ever in their entire lives. When you're out on the streets with no family, no home, what choice do you have? There's nobody to tell you what's right and what's wrong, what's good for you and what's bad for you. Nobody cares. You just do what you have to do, minute to minute, to survive.

It threw me for a loop, meeting folks like that, and realizing that there were so many other people out there in the same position. It wasn't money so much which made me different from them, for I had seen dire poverty in my time. It was the fact that I had a family. People who loved me no matter what, who taught me how to take care of myself and my community and my conscience.

It's love that gives you choices. It's the ties of family that make you feel free.

Before Christmas one year, I did a fund-raising event for Queen of Angels Hospital in California. While I was there, I visited a hospice across the street where there were many people suffering with AIDS. In the courtyard I saw one woman sitting all by herself. I asked about her and was told that her name was Wilma Brown, and that she never had any visitors and acted real rude and bitter to everybody.

So I sat down with Wilma Brown and tried to talk. She was

about thirty, an IV drug user who had contracted AIDS from a needle.

"What do you want?" she said with a hostile glare.

"I'm Jeanne White, Ryan White's mother. Do you know who he was?"

"Yeah. So what?"

"Where are you from?"

"New York."

"You must be lonely way out here without your family."

"I got no family."

"There must be somebody . . ."

"Nope. Been out on the streets alone since I was five."

"Oh. Gosh. Isn't there anyone . . . a friend?"

"I just lost my boyfriend."

"I'm real sorry about that."

"Oh, yeah? Is that so? Well, I don't know why you'd want to sit here and talk to me. I've been a prostitute, I've done drugs, I've sold cocaine, I've been in and out of hospitals and jails my entire life."

"Well, uh . . . we . . . they told me you have a birthday coming up. Would you like for me to send you something for your birthday?"

"Aw, come on, you're not gonna send me nothing for my birthday."

"I promise, Wilma. I will. I promise."

I wanted so much to show her that someone cared about her. As soon as I got home, I sent Wilma Brown a music box, for her birthday and for Christmas both. It arrived at the hospice on December 22. They called and told me that Wilma had died a few days before.

I cried and cried. I told them to give that music box to the next lady with AIDS who showed up there. While I was making our dinner, driving out to an airport, answering mail, the memory of Wilma's ravaged face would come to me and haunt me. It will never leave me.

Grown-ups can't always succeed completely when talking to children. I have learned that sometimes it takes a kid to teach a kid. There's a purity in children's minds, an uncluttered field where a good cause can take root and grow. Maybe with all this talk about how TV has poisoned children's minds, we forget that the media brings children inspiration, too. These days, you don't have to be an educated, experienced adult to see the problem and become involved in its solution. And the ability of young people to communicate with each other, through the media, makes it possible for the young to impact on each other's lives as never before.

When Ryan was alive, he was inspired by a beautiful, articulate young woman from New York, Allie Gertz. She had been infected during her first sexual experience. Ryan and Allie made ABC interactive news broadcasts on laser discs that were acquired by schools so that kids who were listening could talk to them about AIDS. She was an example and mentor to Ryan, another young person striving to bring understanding to the heedless adult world. She put him at his ease. When she died at the age of twenty-six in August 1992, it just tore me up.

After he died, a little five-year-old girl named Jenna Sheffield, from the state of Washington, saw images of Ryan on the news. In the winter of 1990, her mom called and said that Jenna had asked for a special Christmas present—to visit Ryan's grave and say good-bye to him. Although I couldn't really imagine—not having met

Jenna personally—that such a small child should make such a weighty request, I agreed to meet with the Sheffields.

The story turned out to be absolutely true. Jenna is a brilliant child, and she had been captivated by Ryan's story. She had two cabbage patch dolls and named one Ryan, the other Andrea. It sounds like she was obsessed—but no, hers was simply a passionate concern, and now that she's older, Jenna is making good use of it. She has promoted education among the young people in her area for several years and always participates in the Northwest AIDS Walk. She calls me all the time to obtain materials that she then distributes to other kids to make them aware of the dangers of AIDS.

There's another girl I know named Carrie Peter, who contracted AIDS back in 1985 during a summer romance. She joined an HIV/AIDS support group in 1992. There were eleven members—ten men and Carrie. All the men are gone now. She is tireless in her attempts to educate young people about AIDS. Benefiting from this new anti-biotics "cocktail" which is keeping AIDS sufferers in much better shape recently, Carrie goes from school to school, lecturing just as Ryan did, just as I have done.

"You can't sit back and expect things to happen to make life worthwhile," she says. "You have to put something in yourself. Maybe what I'm doing is making a difference to somebody."

It is. I know it. I can see it in my travels—how young people like Carrie and Jenna and Allie Gertz and John Keets and Ryan have changed their generation. Their effort to banish ignorance is an essential ingredient in the AIDS "cocktail." It is the drug that makes all the other drugs work.

Moderation sometimes gets you exactly nowhere. That's an awful hard thing for a well-behaved, straitlaced person to admit, but there it is.

In March 1991, almost a year after Ryan had died, I accepted Larry Kramer's request to be one of the leaders of a six-hundred person march on the White House, spearheaded by the nation's most radical anti-AIDS protest group—ACTUP, the AIDS Coalition to Unleash Power.

ACTUP would do just about anything to get attention. The protesters would throw blood on public officials, burn the flag, prostrate themselves in front of police cars, chant, heckle, break up meetings. The truth is that most gay people are nothing like that. They're not eccentric or hysterical, they behave in a civil, civilized way and they are just as patriotic as I am. Like most of them, I had often turned down invitations to participate in ACTUP demonstrations before. However, there was a time during the Bush Administration when the Ryan White CARE Act was coming up for consideration, and I was so sick to death of the ignorance about AIDS, and so mad at the official silence that surrounded it, that marching with ACTUP looked good to me.

Shelley and I went to Washington. We stayed overnight in a hotel, and in the morning we went downstairs for breakfast. The lobby was crowded with gay men in town for the march. As we were walking through the lobby, four or five guys called out, "Good morning, ladies!" We answered, "Good morning!" thinking that for sure they meant us. Of course, they were really referring to the men walking next to us. We were so embarrassed!

So there we were, me and Shelley Henson, on a sunny day in Washington, D.C., marching along with gays and lesbians and their families and friends and street people and straight people and whoever would agree to march along. I was one of the people holding a banner at the front that said: "120,00 Americans dead of AIDS. Is this your national plan, George?" Shelley was plugging along between a man dressed up as a sexy nurse in spike heels and a street person who smelled like he hadn't seen the wet end of a faucet in about a month.

"Well, hiya, honey," said the street person to Shelley. "This is going to be fun! Last time we did this, they raided us and we got to spend the night in jail and they gave us a free meal!!"

Poor Shelley looked about ready to faint! But she hung in with that old Hoosier spirit and stuck to me like glue. They put me right in front of the White House. Then these fellows fell down at my feet, screaming and writhing. They had splashed fake blood all over themselves to symbolize death by AIDS.

They told me, "You have to padlock yourself to the White House fence! It'll be in all the media! It'll appear on the covers of magazines!"

I said, "Nossir, I will not do any such thing."

Somebody from ACTUP came over and said, "Mrs. White, you'd best get yourself across to the other side of Pennsylvania Avenue right this minute because the cops are coming through here and you're going to end up in jail."

I must say I was very grateful for that advice. No sooner had I taken it than the cops came in and hauled off a lot of folks to the lockup. There were eighty-three arrests.

They burned the flag at the press conference at the rally. I was standing among all these people, and suddenly I turned around and saw a puff of smoke. I thought there must have been an accident. One of the reporters asked me, "Mrs. White, what do you think of ACTUP burning the American flag?"

I was so upset that, for the life of me, I cannot recall what magic power flew into my mind at that moment that made me able to say anything at all. But it has happened to me so often now that I have begun to believe: *The strength you can't imagine you could ever have doesn't just come to you in a flash. It is always there, lying beneath the surface of what you think is your regular old timid personality; and when you need it, you can find it.*

"If you want to call these people radical, then you can call me radical, too," I said. "I'm here to represent moms all across America who are losing their sons and daughters to AIDS. We're tired of not seeing anything done. I know the pain and frustration these people are facing, because I'm facing them, too. All we ask from Mr. Bush is leadership."

You bet I found some of ACTUP's behavior offensive. I hated that they burned the flag, that they yelled obscenities. But I stood my ground. In Kokomo, the moderates often hid behind the radicals, allowing the few so-called crazies to make all the trouble, write the nasty letters, give the belligerent interviews. Then, when public opinion turned against Kokomo, the moderates could say, "It was them. It wasn't really us." I had seen that behavior again and again— my old friend who would say, "It's my husband who doesn't want our kids to play with your kids . . ."; Ryan's school friends who would say, "It's my folks who don't want me to play with you . . ."

I didn't want to be part of that, to let ACTUP do my fighting for me. I told the media: "You get to a point when you can't hardly stand it no more . . . You want to help and you want to do something good; you want to find a cure and to make people listen. But people won't listen."

I ended up with ACTUP because it was the only way to get people to listen. Once your child has AIDS, you are just like everybody else who has met up with the disease. You join forces and fight together and stay alive.

One of the most interesting sidelights of that event happened sometime later. I was making a speech in Kansas and a guy stood up in the audience and asked me, "What did you think of the person who burned the American flag at that rally in Washington?"

"I was very upset about that," I answered.

"It was me," he said.

"Well, I sure did not approve of your behavior," I told him.

Maybe he was just trying to relive the joys of offending an uptight Methodist from Indiana. But I don't think so. I think in his heart he wanted somebody to berate him. Because he felt guilty. All those months afterwards, it was still eating at him.

I had one more experience with Larry Kramer after that. I was on a panel with Larry, Dr. Robert Gallo, the great AIDS physician, and Mary Fisher, who is suffering with AIDS and has done so much wonderful work to combat its spread. It was right on the day that Arthur Ashe had died of AIDS; we were all terribly saddened about that.

At this panel discussion, all of us had spoken again and again about how you could only get AIDS from sexual contact. And somebody asked whether you could get it from mosquitoes. To our astonishment, Dr. Gallo said, "Yes." You could hear the shocked intake of breath in the audience. Then he said, "Of course, to get AIDS from this mosquito, you'd have to have sex with him . . ." Everybody laughed. He sure had us going.

Mary made her presentation. Then I told how I tried to teach young people about AIDS by telling them Ryan's personal story. Then Larry got up and said something nice about Mary. But when he came to me, he said words to the effect that he was sick and tired of hearing about Ryan White.

I was outraged. I felt betrayed. It took all my strength not to burst into tears.

*   *   *

*People write to me and ask: "Why don't you just let Ryan die and go
on with your life?"*

*My answer is: If I let Ryan die, I have to let everybody else who has
this disease die as well. I'm not willing to give up and let these people go.
I would love not to have to talk about Ryan. People don't realize how
draining it is to speak about this subject, how exhausted I get after a
speech, how terrible it is to recall the pain and relive the horror.*

*But there was one person in this country for a time who could really
open people's eyes to the dangers of AIDS, and that was Ryan. He's not
here anymore, so I am trying to continue his work. But I'm not just doing
this for Ryan. I'm doing it for all the people who have had to live and
die with this disease. It would be much easier to quit. But how could I do
that to all the wonderful people who helped me who have passed on? Those
men never gave up. They didn't have to help me. The gay community
never had any obligation to help Jeanne White. But they did. I feel that
if I get out of AIDS education, I'm letting down a lot of people who had
faith in me.*

I've had some incredible times on my travels around this world.

Roy and I went to Alaska together (in 1994, *in February!*), an
exciting trip organized by Alaskans Living With AIDS. I was booked
to make three speeches—in Juneau, Fairbanks and Anchorage—and
they also added Barrow, our city closest to the North Pole, where
the terrain is mostly solid ice and nothing ever grows. At one of
them, I was introduced to a little girl, who later appeared on Phil's
show, who was said to have contracted AIDS from being abused. It
was such a horrible story that it just blew me away.

For two weeks, we drove around on the snow-covered roads,
listening to the silence of the drifts, loving the calm, the isolation,

the peace of the place. One couple in Barrow came over and took us out riding in a dogsled on the ice. The lady lent me a coat, because nobody who isn't a native has a coat that's warm enough for Alaska in February. In Anchorage, Roy took his first skiing lesson. He was just thrilled when he saw a moose by the side of the road. He stopped the car, raced out to take a picture. I was afraid the moose would charge. But luckily, the moose just looked at this guy from Indiana with his camera like he was crazy and went on moseying through the frozen forest.

When the Jewish National Fund flew me and Roy to Israel, we planted trees in Ryan's memory at the AIDS Memorial Forest, part of the Lahav Forest near Beersheba. It was a sad tribute—but a great trip. It impressed me enormously to see such a desert wasteland growing greener and greener, covered with forests and fields because of the efforts of the Jewish National Fund. Our group included ten people from all across America who started out as strangers and became the closest of friends. We had a fabulous time. We toured all the ancient, historic sites. Our group passed by this wedding in Tel Aviv and we were invited to come right in and join the fun. Our thoughtful hosts got together a special tour for us of the Christian holy places, including the Way of the Cross in Jerusalem.

A mystery was solved for us in Israel. When we visited the monument to those who had been murdered in the Holocaust, we saw that the memorial markers were heaped with stones—and we realized suddenly that the stones which kept appearing on Ryan's grave at home were not just tossed there by the weather but deliberately placed there by Jewish people as a sign that they had visited and paid their respects.

In Birmingham, my sister, Janet, and her husband, Leo, arranged for me to appear at an AIDS benefit hosted by Joan Rivers. (When we were kids, it used to get me crazy that Janet was so beautiful and athletic. But now, when I see that she's still beautiful and athletic, it makes me just as proud as I can be.) The event was elegant and dignified and we raised quite a bit of money to further the battle against AIDS in Alabama. When *Good Housekeeping* magazine made me one of their Women of the Year, I felt as though I had entered the finest company in the land. I was tremendously honored to receive the Helen Hayes Award along with Annette Funicello, my high school idol, who has suffered with multiple sclerosis and become a spokesperson for other people living with that disease. Frankie Avalon was supposed to be there, but he couldn't make it, so Bobby Rydell came in his place. These people *were* my teenage years. I was in Heaven! I felt like I was on *American Bandstand* with Dick Clark!

A great milestone for Ryan occurred on December 1, 1990, when he posthumously received the NAACP Image Award. I went to the ceremonies with Greg Louganis to accept the award on Ryan's behalf. There I was, surrounded by all these famous, brilliant black entertainers, standing in for my son, who because of his own suffering had reached across the gulf that divides the races and become a person whom the African-American community wanted to honor. Sandra J. Evers-Manly of the Beverly Hills/Hollywood NAACP explained that Ryan was being honored because his "legacy as a champion of the rights of those afflicted with the AIDS virus, regardless of color or creed, will stand as a benchmark for generations to come."

Roy and I went to Washington in October 1992 to see the great AIDS quilt spread out on the Capitol green, 22,000 panels that each measured three feet by six feet and commemorated the lives of some Americans felled by AIDS. There were dozens of panels dedicated to Ryan. I remember one from *The Home Show;* one from the school in Statesville, North Carolina, where we had made our movie; another made by the folks on the *Geraldo* show, where Phil Donahue and I had appeared to commemorate the tenth anniversary of the AIDS epidemic; another made by my mother that hangs in our Ryan White Foundation office today and says "Gone Too Soon." We wandered among the weeping survivors, in this meadow of remembrances. Roy tried to take a picture of each of Ryan's panels, but it was too much, we couldn't even walk that far and in October 1997 when we went back to visit the quilt, 3,000 more panels had been added. It stretched from the capital to the Lincoln Memorial.

What a monument that quilt is! It must be preserved for all time, as a reminder of our country's loss.

I've been asked on several occasions to lead church services. I felt very nervous about that—like God was going to hear me real good this time, so I'd better not mess up. One church wanted me to focus on the idea of guardian angels, which has come to have so much significance in these unsettled and dangerous days. The other church wanted me to focus on discrimination. They were both open churches that let everybody in—black and white, gay and straight. These congregations wanted to understand how to resist the impulse to make anyone an outcast. Standing in those pulpits, I felt so loved and loving, so accepted and accepting.

My whole way of thinking about what a church should be has changed. I used to belong to churches where everyone was the same. Now I believe in churches that accept everybody, no matter how "different" he or she is. Church for me now must be open, inclusive, small enough so each member of the congregation feels known and counted.

I used to believe I knew exactly what was and was not a sin. Now I am not so sure that I'm the one who ought to be making that judgment.

195

There have been some occasions on which I would have given anything not to represent a child who had become famous. I dreaded the radio call-in shows. They bring you on and you expect you're going to be able to give your message, and then they've got a whole squad of hate callers all lined up to wish you dead on the airwaves, saying, "Lady, there's a place where homosexuals go, it's the place where sinners go, and so will you for defending them." In St. Louis, I had these people calling in, saying I was a front for the gay community, attacking me for recommending the use of condoms. One man said he didn't feel he had to pay for helping anybody with AIDS because he was just a poor taxpayer and had never slept with anybody he shouldn't have slept with, so why was he responsible?

Like Ryan in his earliest TV appearances, I gave one-word answers and let it go at that. I couldn't wait to get off the phone. I told the announcer: "There's some people you're never going to be able to change."

With some of these shows, the controversy is always more important than the truth. They don't care what the truth is; they're not after the truth; they're after a nice, bloody fight. The radio folks often wanted me to holler back at these people. But I never do. When I went on the media shows, it was because I wanted to get my story across. I didn't want the truth of what I had to say denied or debated; I didn't want to have to be more brilliant and articulate than some minister who thought I was a sinner and a liar, because the likelihood was that I could never be that.

It's a terrible thing to feel you've been lured into a trap, that you've been invited just to be sacrificed. It makes you distrustful; it makes you hate the media; it takes all your strength to go back out there and do those shows again.

I will never be an actress. It'll never be my thing. If ever you've been tempted to look at somebody like my friend the late Lee Mathis appearing on my favorite soap opera, General Hospital, *and say, "Hey, I can do that!"—well, think again. I had maybe thirty words to say on* General Hospital *once and I totally freaked. Years and years of media appearances, and I fear I'll always be a basket case in front of the cameras.*

It started with *The Home Show,* Ryan's last appearance on television. The public relations man for that show was Scott Barton. We became very good friends. At Scott's urging, I did *The Home Show* several times after Ryan died. He talked me into going to this benefit for AIDS in Atlanta called ARTCARE, in which talented artists donated their works to be auctioned off to benefit AIDS patients in their city. There I met Scott's friend Dr. Will Idsten. Both Scott and Will came to my wedding, along with many other friends from the gay community.

I'd do anything for Scott. Anything at all. Except one time he asked me to do something that was just too much. He had become the public relations man at *General Hospital* and the folks there were sitting around, trying to think whom they could invite for the segment at the Annual Nurses' Ball for AIDS Awareness in June 1995. Somebody suggested that maybe I could appear. Scott said, "Sure! I'll get Jeanne! I know her real well! I was at her wedding."

They gave me four lines to memorize. Four lines! But I was a helpless mass of nerves at the idea of saying them on camera in front of millions of Americans. Roy rehearsed them with me all day, but naturally, when they turned on the camera, I fluffed. Thank Heaven for the miracle of tape!

*   *   *

People don't fool me like they used to. Now that I've had to read so many strange situations, I've gotten really good at smelling a hint of trouble, trusting my instinct that something may be wrong.

In November 1993, Roy and I went out to Los Angeles where the Athletes and Entertainers for Kids were honoring Greg Louganis. I was going to present Greg with a sculpture of Ryan that Bill Mack had done. The event was held at Taco Bell headquarters. I said a few words and presented Greg with the sculpture, and no sooner had I done that than he reached into his pocket and *presented me* with a medal.

I said to myself: *What's going on here? This wasn't in the script.*

Greg told the crowd that our family had been his true friends and supporters for many years, that he had learned an enormous amount from Ryan and that he really wanted me to have one of the gold medals he had won at the Olympics in Seoul, Korea. He put it around my neck. He had given his Pan American Games medal and a national championship medal to Ryan, but he was giving this to me, he said, because he really wanted me to have a medal all for myself. I was just overwhelmed. I couldn't hold back the tears.

After that, we spent the whole evening together, but he didn't seem himself. I said to Roy, "Something is wrong, something is really bothering him, I can feel it, like he wants to tell me something . . ."

He told Roy that in his new book, *Breaking the Surface,* I might read something I wouldn't be happy about. We wondered what that would be. I began to worry. He didn't tell me he had AIDS. But I kind of suspected. Then, in January 1994, he went on Barbara Walters's show, and the truth came out.

On a Sunday night at midnight, I received a call from the *Oprah*

Winfrey show. They were having Greg as a guest the next day and wanted me to be on the show as a surprise for him. I said I didn't know if I could because Mom was coming in and we were going to go out for breakfast and then go shopping together. She was looking forward to this little break because she had been home for weeks taking care of my brother, Tommy Joe, who was ill with cancer, while his wife went to work. I hated to ruin Mom's day when she needed me so much.

The folks at *Oprah* very kindly told me to bring her along.

We got up way before dawn to make the show. It was a complete surprise for Greg, and apparently a relief for him as well, because— just as I had sensed that night in Los Angeles—he had been very concerned about how I would react to the news that he was ill.

Thank Heaven Greg is still well and strong today. I keep the gold medal in a place of honor among my most precious possessions.

My dear brother, Tommy Joe Hale, who had blessed me with the strength of his faith all through our hard times, took sick with cancer in 1988. Four years later, in 1992, it was in remission and he was feeling fine. So I took the opportunity to invite him to come with me to Los Angeles, where Judith Light and some other show-business people were having a fund-raiser featuring a play called *Heart Strings* to raise consciousness about AIDS.

It was such a pleasure to see quiet, gentle Tom looking so hand-some, in his tuxedo, smiling and shaking hands with all these good Hollywood folks. I was so proud of him. We took a three-day vacation together and had the best time, sightseeing and touring around. It brought back memories of when we were kids up at Bruce Lake, hunting for bait and playing cards and eating fresh fish grilled on Mom's fire.

Weeding Out The Tears

When Tom died—on May 12, 1995, of non-Hodgkin's lymphoma—all the family came in for the funeral. But I kept thinking: *Now, why couldn't we have had this reunion when Tommy was alive?* He would have had such a grand time with all the cousins and his kids and their kids and their memories. Why do we let this greatest of supports—our families—slip away, when we need them so much in good times and bad?

My mom and I, who were always close, have been drawn even closer by this experience, for she has lost her only son as I lost mine. She has a statue of a little angel driving a car, and another angel hitching a ride to Heaven. She thinks of the driver as Ryan and the hitchhiker as his beloved uncle Tom. I believe she's right, that these two men whom our family lost have become angels for us, waiting in Heaven, beaming at us with their persistent love, lighting our way.

I have tried to stop being a pushover . . . but truthfully, I have failed. Somehow I never managed to get myself enrolled in those assertiveness-training courses that were so popular for a while. It always takes somebody else to save me from being taken advantage of. We wimps need protectors. Ryan White was one of the best. Andrea White is right up there. So is Shelley Henson.

Roy Ginder takes the gold.

At one of my speaking engagements when Roy was with me, our hosts prevailed upon me to make an additional, unscheduled appearance. When I said okay, they stuck us out in a motel in the middle of nowhere with no car and no way to get ourselves some dinner, and then picked us up bright and early and expected me to make yet another unscheduled television appearance.

I would have said, "Yes."

But my husband, Roy, said, "No way. She's not doing one more thing until we have some breakfast."

"But they're waiting at the station . . ." insisted our chaperons.

"I'm really sorry about that," Roy said. "But they'll just have to wait a little longer. You can't invite people to come and address your audience and then treat them without consideration. Now, how about that breakfast?"

In Kansas City, the local anti-AIDS activists were having a tough time getting the gay community involved. When I visited there, I was asked to walk down this strip and stop in at these gay bars and try to convince the folks inside to join us in our attempts to awaken the community to the dangers of AIDS.

We were getting a little bit tired, and Roy said, "Come on, hon, let's stop and sit down for a while."

The leaders of the march suggested that we stop at a motel. You could see immediately that it was a gay motel. Roy and I were taken to this room, and to my amazement, the whole bed was spread with what looked like thousands of condoms. They asked me to sit on the bed so they could take pictures. I guess it was somebody's idea of good publicity. Personally, I thought it was a pretty stupid idea. My husband reacted more seriously and just about hit the ceiling. That was the end of that photo opportunity.

At a restaurant in upstate New York, after an appearance for the Ryan White Foundation, a bunch of people came after me and insisted that I support this politician who was running for President—Bill Clinton.

I said, "Fellas, let me tell you, you've got to kind of watch what you say in front of Roy here, because he's a Rush Limbaugh fan."

They shut up real quick. However, that event made me a fan of Bill Clinton, because as far as I could see, he was one of the first politicians to come out and actively seek the endorsement of well-known AIDS activists like me. When the late Elizabeth Glaser spoke at the Democratic convention, and described how she and her children had contracted AIDS, my heart broke—but I also knew we had reached a new turning point in American political life when AIDS was acknowledged as a national enemy, and its defeat became a common cause. When President Clinton was inaugurated, Roy and I went to Washington to hear Michael Jackson sing a new song he had written that honored Ryan: "Gone Too Soon." It was Clinton's way of saying he was on Ryan's side, and Michael's way of saying he would never forget.

Eventually the Ryan White Foundation settled into larger offices donated by the Merchants' Plaza in downtown Indianapolis. Betsy Stewart volunteered as executive director, and was succeeded by Melinda Mains. Now we have moved out to West 86th Street and Judy Burnett has become executive director. Under Judy's leadership, the foundation—the only national foundation to focus exclusively on HIV/AIDS education—has grown so much that Michael Morrison and Lynn Becker are now on staff full-time, and we have many part-timers and regular volunteers. We have given out Angel Awards to tireless crusaders against AIDS. Glamorous, generous friends like Lorna Luft and Diana Canova have become our supporters. Christopher Radko, the brilliant glass artist, makes a beautiful Christmas ornament every year to remember the victims of AIDS, and part of the proceeds of the sale of the ornaments goes to our foundation. Great corporations have helped us. The Hyatt Regency has hosted some of our guests. Pizza Hut gave us a large cash gift in honor of Ryan's being named to the National Geographic Kids' Hall of Fame. Phil Donahue and Greg Louganis literally auctioned the shirts off their backs after a benefit polo match one year. Thousands of plain, ordinary people have helped us with donations. They know that the work we do is life-saving.

Our mandate is to educate youth about the dangers of AIDS. I go everywhere I can with my *57th Street* and *Gone Too Soon* tapes and my speech that changes every time I give it.

I've tried my best to publicize former Surgeon General C. Everett Koop's advice to young lovers: "Find someone who is worthy of your respect and love, give that person both and stay faithful to him or her. In other words, short of total abstention, the best defense against AIDS is to maintain a faithful monogamous relationship."

But I know that it's often not so simple. We have seen too many young women who tried to prevent themselves from getting pregnant by having oral sex or anal sex and years later, when they're ready to have children, find out they're HIV-positive. We've seen too many men who contracted HIV in prison, where there were no condoms available, and then went back to their straight lives on the outside and infected people they loved.

The foundation focuses on why we must educate our youth. Teenagers think they are invulnerable. The "It Can't Happen To Me" syndrome is common. Yet one in four new HIV infections occurs in people younger than twenty-two.

Young people are having sex earlier than ever. Seventy percent of teens have had sex by their senior year in high school, often with multiple partners. Especially vulnerable are teens who are runaways, youth offenders, homeless and migrant youth. But *all* young people who are having sex and using IV drugs may be at risk. It's not who they are but what they do that puts them at risk for HIV and AIDS.

Anybody who thinks that explicit, frank information about sexual activity isn't necessary for his children is simply ignoring the facts and risking his children's lives. (When I go out and address kids, *fifth-graders* ask me about condoms!) In the fall after Ryan died, I remember, I went to make a speech at the PTA in Lincoln, Nebraska. They invited me because they had seen some alarming statistics. The Nebraska Prevention Center for Alcohol and Drug Abuse had done a survey that showed that 77 percent of twelfth-grade girls and 66 percent of twelfth-grade boys had had sex in the past year, about 30 percent of each gender with multiple partners. They're not any more liberal in Nebraska than anyplace else, but figures like that would give anybody pause.

I always say to the kids when I talk to them: "You'd like to think that I'm not having sex, wouldn't you? You'd like to think that your parents aren't having sex either." And the kids laugh, and they go, "Oh, my God, gross me out!" And I say, "But listen here, we *are* having sex. And we always know what we're doing, but we never can be absolutely sure what somebody else is doing. You don't come to us and say, 'Mom and Dad, I'm having sex.' So we have to assume that you are. That's why education is so important. You have to be responsible for your own self. You have a choice now whether to get AIDS. My Ryan—who would have been twenty-five this year—did not have a choice. Have sex when you're ready, not when somebody else wants you to. You stay in control."

That is why education on AIDS is so important in the lives of young people. Because they are not going to step forward and ask for advice. It has to be given to them in a form in which they will accept it, soon enough to be useful to them and to protect them. Mrs. Hillary Rodham Clinton agreed with us about the need to educate. The R.W.F. named her Health Educator of the Year in 1995, and the remarks she made at that time are part of a video we value greatly.

A lot of kids today have single parents. "You might have to be the one who educates your parents," I tell them. "The best thing you can do if you hear something incorrect about AIDS—if you hear somebody say it can be gotten from tears, sweat or saliva—is to be the teacher and correct those people."

I try to make the kids see that every time they have sex with somebody, they have sex with all the people that person has had sex with. Look how many people a person could have sex with in fifteen years. And think of what it would be like to have to go back and find those people and tell them you've been infected, and then they'd have to go back and tell all the other people they had sex with after you! The numbers are just enormous.

Even the kids who think they know everything can't beat those numbers.

Today at the Ryan White Foundation, we realize that we can't focus only on HIV/AIDS. We have to talk about teen pregnancy (a million teenagers get pregnant every year) and sexually transmitted diseases (one in four Americans get one by age twenty-one); we have to talk about violence, and about drug and alcohol abuse—because all of these issues follow alongside the AIDS epidemic and increase the risk to our young people.

We try to keep young people safe from HIV/AIDS by:

- Increasing understanding and acceptance of people with HIV/AIDS through education.
- Informing and educating target populations and community groups about HIV/AIDS.
- Providing grants for HIV/AIDS education programs conceived and implemented by youth.

- Developing and implementing an HIV/AIDS peer education program on a national basis.
- Hosting an annual national youth conference for peer educators, ages fourteen to twenty-three.
- Providing age-appropriate educational materials for use by schools and community-based organizations.

Our teens are our future. We must do whatever it takes to save their lives.

If you raise a child with love and discipline, if you give that child everything you can, then eventually you have to sit back and trust that what you have done is enough and your child will come through okay. That's what happened to me and my daughter, Andrea.

The loss of privacy which had accompanied Ryan's fame just haunted her. She blew off anybody who wanted to talk to her, demanding isolation, anonymity.

Meanwhile, she couldn't figure out what she wanted to do with her life.

She was accepted into Indiana University and we took her to Bloomington with high hopes. But then she decided it was too much for her, that she didn't like the dorm, didn't want to be away from home while I was starting my new marriage, didn't want to leave the house her brother had built to a new family of folks she hardly knew, and so she moved back. She got a job with the local newspaper. She worked as a security guard at the museum. She decided what she really wanted to do was to become a policewoman, and went down to Alabama to take a test. But then, to her great disappointment (and my secret joy), she didn't qualify to take the test and gave up the whole idea and came home. Then she decided to join the Marines. That idea fell through as well.

She was uneasy about my marriage, uneasy about my job. I was scared to death that she would marry somebody when she was way too young, just as I had, and find herself in domestic hell, the way I had. I was scared she would get in with a fast crowd and buy real trouble.

But the basic strength of her character held her down to earth. Like my own mother, powerless to help in a time of crisis, I simply had to hold my breath and pray that she would come safely through the storms. And she has. My Andrea will be twenty-four years old in October 1997. She is finishing her degree at I.U.P.U.I. (Indiana University-Purdue University at Indianapolis) and working as an administrative assistant. She writes a column for our foundation newsletter and volunteers regularly at the foundation office.

I believe that Andrea must have worlds to speak about the terrible problems of the well sibling, but the worlds are silent still. Maybe someday she will understand how important it might be to share her experience with other kids who have wondered why fate has selected them to be okay while a suffering brother or sister slips away. For the time being, she wants her privacy. She wants the past to fade and let her be.

Sometimes you wonder whether it's worth it. You worry that Roy is maybe feeling kind of lonesome, that Andrea's off someplace investigating a new career idea. You say to yourself: Now, what am I doing here ten million miles from home when I need to be with my family? And then the answer comes. Somehow the answer always comes.

*   *   *

Kevin Neal is a gay man who organized a wonderful local group called Metro Teen AIDS in Washington, D.C. He had the help of a gallant physician, Dr. Lawrence D'Angelo, a physician at Children's Hospital who treats lots of infected kids and now serves on the Honorary Board of the Ryan White Foundation.

I met Kevin because he called and asked me to do an event to help raise money for infected teenagers in the D.C. area. For many years, he and his associates had been giving youth service awards in Ryan's name.

While I was in Washington, Kevin asked me to visit a friend of his who was in the hospital. This young man—about thirty—was terribly depressed. He didn't want to comb his hair or brush his teeth or receive visitors. He just wanted to lie there and die as quickly as possible.

I stood outside the hospital room. The nurse went in to tell the young man I was there to see him. And to my astonishment, I heard him say, "No! Absolutely not! She can't come in here until I have fixed myself up! I have to brush my teeth, comb my hair! *Please don't let Mrs. White come in here until I have combed my hair!*"

I was so thrilled. It wasn't that I was flattered that a visit from me could mean so much. It was that I felt so validated in my work, so satisfied that it was worth all this trouble, that these people who had pushed me out there on the road were not just making up stories to motivate me but were really telling the truth.

I had made the right decision.

I *could* make a difference.

People ask me how I feel about being "famous." I don't feel like I'm famous and I wouldn't want to be—I've seen too much of how the really famous people like Elton and Michael long for a private moment, a moment with family.

No, I want to be a private person, coming and going as I please. If anything, I'd like people to say, "Jeanne White? She was a good mother who had great kids, and she ended up fulfilling one of her lifelong ambitions—she became a teacher."

Chapter 9

Part of America's Progress

Of course, AIDS is off the front pages now. Magic Johnson announced he had HIV in November 1991 and retired, expecting never to return to basketball. Five years later, he's playing again, because his physicians have learned to handle AIDS, to treat it as a chronic disease. But it's wise to remember that a millionaire athlete finds it a lot easier to get all the drugs and all the care he needs than those who are less well set financially. People who contract AIDS still face ruin, as well as death, and the organizations that are out there trying to help them still need funding, and the people who want AIDS patients cast away like garbage are still in positions of great power.

On June 28, 1995, at the Washington Hilton Hotel, there was an annual meeting of the Title I and Title II grantees, and Greg Louganis and I gave out awards to HIV/AIDS care providers Hank Carde, Luigi Ferrer, Storm Jecker, Kioshi Kuromiya, Bill Lotero and Steven Land. We were meeting at a critical time, when reauthorization of the Ryan White CARE Act was in deep jeopardy. Anita Eichler, Director of the Division of HIV Services (DHS), explained that the fight for reauthorization was now at a crossroads of government reorganization, political change, fiscal constraints and an imminent overhaul in the health-care system.

The reauthorization bill was sponsored by Senator Kennedy and Senator Nancy Kassebaum of Kansas. It would provide medical and support services, AZT and other drugs, home nursing and out-patient care to the hundreds of thousands of people who were now living with HIV. One poll showed that 77 percent of Americans wanted more funding to help people with AIDS. The vast majority of the Congress—including House Speaker Newt Gingrich—supported reauthorization. However, it was being stymied by Senator Jesse Helms of North Carolina. I thought of his delaying tactics as "The Kokomo Offense"—hold things up long enough and death will come and the whole problem will un-happen.

In July 1995, Senator Helms said he opposed the reauthorization for the Ryan White CARE Act because he said people with AIDS had gotten sick "as a result of deliberate, disgusting, revolting conduct." He said: "We've got to have some common sense about a disease transmitted by people deliberately engaging in unnatural acts." And he added that he felt AIDS was receiving a disproportionate amount of funding. I didn't agree. At that time, heart disease was receiving $3.6 billion in federal funding; cancer, $16.9 billion.

And AIDS, then and now the leading cause of death among adults twenty-four to forty-four, received about six billion dollars.

The media asked what I thought about what Senator Helms had said. I told them I thought his statements were sad and crazy. Everybody who has sex runs the risk of getting AIDS. And that may even include the good Senator himself. This is not a homosexual disease; it is a people disease.

Should we let people who have lung cancer suffer and die untended because somebody thinks smoking is a nasty habit?

Should we lose our compassion for people who have cirrhosis of the liver because they may have contracted it from drinking too much?

Just for the sake of discussion, turn the political tables a little. Remember all the soldiers who came home from Vietnam with ailments incurred because of exposure to Agent Orange? Should they have been ignored and despised because some people thought the war was immoral?

Whoever starts singling out groups of sick people to abandon on the basis of some so-called moral consideration enters a spiral of inhumanity and evil conscience. I say Senator Helms and those who think like him have a lot of nerve telling any mother that her child's life is less precious than that of any other ailing citizen. Every time the bill comes up for new funding, it has to be passed—until this terrible plague of AIDS is conquered and the sick are made well.

Thank Heaven the U.S. Congress agreed with me and passed the five-year reauthorization in 1996.

The first time the Ryan White CARE Act was signed into law, President Bush was relaxing at Kennebunkport, Maine, and there wasn't too much publicity. But in 1996, there was a different president and a different attitude. Patricia Fleming, the Director of the National Office of AIDS Policy, called and said that the reauthorization bill was going to be signed in Washington on May 27, and she invited me to be there.

It was a wonderful reunion for me. More than forty people were there—representatives of all these different AIDS organizations who had helped to run the lobbying campaign.

Somebody came over to me and said, "Mrs. White, we'll be taking you into the Oval Office. There you will meet Mr. Clinton. Then we'll go into the Roosevelt Room [where all my colleagues and the media people were waiting] for the signing of the bill. Mr. Clinton always enters the room first. You are to follow him, one step behind and to the right, and make sure you're standing close enough to him to get in all the pictures. Then he will go to his desk and sign the Ryan White CARE Act, and you just stand behind him."

I nodded and smiled politely, but inside, I was frantic. I kept thinking: *What is Jeanne White from Kokomo, Indiana, doing here at the White House?! This is crazy! This can't be happening!* I was just so astounded by the whole thing that nervousness seemed beside the point. In the hallway outside the Oval Office, I remember wondering why it wasn't as fancy as I had imagined, and noting that the walls could have used a coat of paint. The Secret Service lurked everywhere around. They were so serious that you just felt totally dumb if you smiled and said hi. I didn't know what I was going to find when I got into that Oval Office, but I was sure it would probably be a surprise.

It was. The Oval Office is a lot bigger than I ever thought it was—and President Clinton is a lot better-looking. He often looks so tired out in pictures, you forget what a young, energetic man he is until you meet him. He told me, "You had a mighty fine son,

Mrs. White. He really put a face to this disease and helped educate everybody on AIDS."

Then he started walking, so I walked behind him like I had been told. He turned and gave me this big smile.

I said, "I'm not supposed to be following you yet, am I?"

He laughed. Turned out he was just going to adjust his tie.

Finally they were ready for us. President Clinton gave a wonderful speech. At one point he looked at me and said:

"Your fine son became a hero to many of us. He was a brave young man who taught America the truth about AIDS. He helped people all over the world to understand that people with AIDS deserve not only the best medical care but also our compassion and our love. And we're eternally grateful for that."

After so much silence, so much ignorance and neglect, it overjoyed me to hear the President of the United States acknowledge the great struggle of those who had suffered with AIDS and those who had struggled to take care of them:

> "It's hard to believe, but AIDS has now been with us for nearly two decades.
>
> "In that time, more than half a million Americans have been diagnosed; more than three hundred thousand of our fellow citizens have died. AIDS has taken too many friends and relatives and loved ones from every one of us in this room. It has shaken the faith of many, but it has inspired a remarkable community spirit . . . At one time AIDS was thought of as inevitably the end of life, the death of hope. But today, through the twin miracles of science and spirit . . . there is hope for a cure.
>
> "We know that AIDS affects all Americans. Every

person with HIV or AIDS is someone's son or daughter, brother or sister, parent or grandparent. We cannot allow discrimination of any kind to blind us to what we must do. The Ryan White CARE Act has been part of America's progress. Since it became law in 1990, this bill has helped hundreds of thousands of people to get the care they need in clinics and doctors' offices. It's kept people out of hospitals so they could be cared for at home, surrounded by families and loved ones. It's paid for the growing assortment of promising drugs that are helping so many people with AIDS to live longer and healthier lives . . . Half the people who are infected get their care through the Ryan White CARE Act . . .

"But even as we celebrate our progress, we shouldn't forget that the fight is not over . . . Until there is a cure, we cannot and must not rest. . . . In his autobiography, Ryan White describes himself as 'just another kid from Kokomo.' We know he was much more than that. He taught a nation to care instead of hate, to embrace people living with AIDS as a part of our American family, to extend always the hand of hope. . . .

"This legislation offers hope for another five years. Let us all pray that no President will ever have to sign another bill, because by then we will have found a cure for AIDS."

When the President finished his speech, he sat down to sign the act, with all the Senators and Representatives who had sponsored it standing behind him—Senator Kassebaum of Kansas, my old friend Senator Orrin Hatch, Senator Bill Frist of Tennessee, Congressman

Steve Gunderson of Wisconsin, Congressman Henry Waxman and Congresswoman Nancy Pelosi of California. I was sorry that Secretary Donna Shalala and Senator Ted Kennedy, who had provided so much leadership on the AIDS issue, could not be there to share in that moment. It pained me more than I can say that Terry Beirn and Mike Callan and so many other hard-fighting Americans had not lived to see this day. I was so overcome with pride and joy and sadness all at the same time that I just reached down and put my hand on the President's shoulder like I was his mother or something.

His staff people thought that was real funny. "In the entire history of the Republic," they said, laughing, "that has to be the first time anybody at a bill signing has rested a hand on the President's shoulder."

He had all these pens lined up around the bill and with each pen he signed one letter of his name and then that pen was given to one of the people who had sponsored the bill. There was one pen left over. After the ceremony someone tried to take it. Mr. Clinton said, "No. We'll give this to Senator Kennedy."

Then he turned around and gave me the first pen. I thanked him and all the people who had worked on the bill. It was the most glorious moment for me. I just wish Ryan had been there, to feel that he was "part of America's progress," to see how much his life meant to his country.

But on second thought, I guess he *was* there.

When Ryan was ill, I had no time for gardening. Now every single day I work in my yard. I plant tomatoes, blackberries, strawberries, roses and lilies, and a few kinds of annuals and perennials. Early in the morning, just at that hour when I used to get up and fill the sink and get my son's medicines ready, I go out there and start up the day in my garden. I flip the Japanese beetles off the roses into a jar of water and cooking oil. I feed the two pretty fish in my pond, and trim off all the browning leaves and flower heads. We have three raccoons who empty my bird feeders every night, so in the morning I fill up the feeders again, and when that's done I give myself a laugh by singing out "Ring-a-ding-ding!" so the birds know their breakfast is ready. I mix a cup of water and a fourth of a cup of sugar and fill up the hummingbird feeders. Soon they're out whirring around me, as beautiful as the flowers whose nectar they love.

The dawn is like my state of mind these days. I look forward to everything. I love being married. Roy has made my life fun again. I look forward to every minute with him, to a long future, to growing old. Andrea has grown into a strong, smart, beautiful person. I look forward to everything her life has in store for us—adventures, travels, grandchildren. On the edge of the sky just beyond a cloud, I think I really see the end of the plague of AIDS. Every day, people whose lives once seemed to be finished are bursting with new health. The cure is coming. It's almost here. I feel like I will live to see it.

What greater gift can anyone receive than this sense of happy anticipation?

The garden has been my therapy. It's my other season besides Christmas. Here among the flowers and the bright fruit, when the light is brand new and everything is fresh and wet and the leaves are beaded up with dewdrops, I work in the household of nature and refresh my spirit.

In that lovely garden, I know exactly what my dad felt out on the lake under the shooting stars. I am sure, just as he was, that "there's got to be a better Being someplace behind all this." It seems to me that every weed I pull is a bit of grief I am learning to set aside, a tear I've weeded out so that good cheer can grow again.

I see in the faces of the flowers all the friends I have lost; I see my son's face. They are beautiful in the new morning, opening like smiles, and shining with hope.

Thank you, Lord, for another day.

Appendix

Every year, the Ryan White Foundation gives out Angel Awards to individuals, companies and institutions that have made extraordinary contributions to the fight against AIDS.

Ryan's Angel Awards—1994 and 1995

JUDITH LIGHT—Actress and star of *Who's the Boss?*; portrayed Jeanne White in *The Ryan White Story*. Judith has given ongoing support for the fight against AIDS, volunteering to help such organizations as The NAMES Project, AIDS Project Los Angeles, Project Angel Food, AmFAR, Mastery Foundation and the Ryan White Foundation. A member of the RWF Honorary Board.

CARRIE PETER—young Missouri woman who contracted AIDS from her boyfriend and now spends her time speaking and raising consciousness about AIDS among high school and college students.

HAL LASTER—a university professor who completed a 3,220-mile cross-country bicycle trip from Disneyland to Disney World to benefit the Ryan White Foundation.

CONRAD KUCZYNSKI and CONTINENTAL OFFICE FURNITURE AND SUPPLY—donated office supplies to the Ryan White Foundation in its early start-up years.

KIMBALL INTERNATIONAL—donated office furniture to the Ryan White Foundation.

MCI—underwrote the Ryan White Foundation long-distance phone for the first year of its existence.

COMPASS MANAGEMENT AND LEASING—gave the Ryan White Foundation office space at Merchants' Plaza.

LEANZA CORNETT—Miss America 1993 and former *Entertainment Tonight* correspondent, Leanza increased awareness of HIV and AIDS during her reign as Miss America by speaking out about AIDS to the nation and showing compassion to those infected with and affected by HIV and AIDS.

BRIAN AUSTIN GREEN—actor and singer, currently starring in *Beverly Hills 90210*. Brian is a member of the Honorary Board of Directors of the Ryan White Foundation. He has volunteered his time repeatedly to help the foundation in its AIDS awareness and fund-raising activities.

GREG LOUGANIS—Olympic gold medalist in diving; actor and author. Greg was a friend of Ryan's during his life and has remained a friend to Jeanne and to the Ryan White Foundation. Greg's bestseller, *Breaking the Surface*, has increased understanding and acceptance of those living with HIV and AIDS. Greg has volunteered his time on many occasions to raise funds for the foundation and dedicated his book to Ryan. He is a member of the RWF Honorary Board.

WOODROW MYERS, M.D.—was the first Chairman of the Board of the Ryan White Foundation. Dr. Myers is a nationally known leader in the field of HIV and AIDS. He is the former Health Commissioner for the Indiana State Board of Health, former Commissioner of Health for New York City, and has served on the Board of Directors for the National Community AIDS Partnership, the American Foundation for AIDS Research, and the National Leadership Coalition on AIDS. He served as Vice-Chairman of the President's Commission on the HIV Epidemic.

METRO TEEN AIDS—a Washington D.C.-based youth organization, Metro Teen AIDS has been on the forefront of HIV/AIDS education for adolescents. MTA is committed to preventing a future for the AIDS epidemic among youth by providing outreach services and peer education, and dispensing quality care and referrals to young people who are infected. MTA annually awards the Ryan White Youth Service Award to honor those who have made notable contributions in the fight against adolescent infection.

HAMILTON HEIGHTS HIGH SCHOOL—set the standard for HIV/AIDS education among schools when it prepared the parents and student body for Ryan White's attendance at Hamilton Heights. The principal, faculty and student government approached Ryan's situation with compassion, understanding and education. Hamilton Heights serves as a role model for all schools.

CLAY JUNIOR HIGH SCHOOL—the student body of this junior high took it upon themselves to raise money for the Ryan White Foundation. By placing jars in the cafeteria for spare change and by selling AIDS ribbons, the young people raised more than $1,000 for the foundation's AIDS education efforts. Clay proved that kids can make a difference.

TERRE HAUTE NORTH WINTERGUARD—this high school flag corps developed a program with an AIDS-awareness theme. The costumes, flags, readings and quilt panels brought attention to the AIDS pandemic in a unique and thoughtful way.

THE JUNIOR LEAGUE OF INDIANAPOLIS—has been a partner of the Ryan White Foundation for the past four years and has provided both financial support and a phenomenal volunteer base to enable the foundation to grow and develop much more quickly than would have been possible without their help.

KATHY MARTIN HARRISON—1995 "Volunteer of the Year"; be-
came involved with the Foundation when the RWF approached the
Junior League for assistance. She co-chaired the League's Ryan
White Committee, now serves as a member of the Foundation's
Board of Directors as chair of the Development Committee, is a
part-time volunteer staff member and chaired the 1995 Ryan's Angel
Awards celebration.

Ryan's Angel Awards—1996

PHIL DONAHUE—has used the television talk show format he pion-
eered in 1967 to focus attention on the AIDS crisis in America. In
1988, a *Donahue* special, "Ryan White Talks to Kids About AIDS,"
provided Ryan a national forum in which to speak to young people
just like him. In 1991, Donahue became the founding chairperson
of the Ryan White Foundation and today continues his efforts to
support the foundation in its work. Phil Donahue has been honored
with more than twenty Daytime Emmy Awards, including a Lifetime
Achievement Award presented in 1996.

MARLO THOMAS—award-winning actress, television producer and
activist, has supported the work of the Ryan White Foundation since
its inception. She is a member of the RWF Honorary Board.

MARTIN KEILMAN, M.D.—a pediatric infectious disease specialist;
was Ryan's doctor during his illness and continues to treat HIV/
AIDS children from throughout Indiana. He has repeatedly volunteered his time and efforts in support of the foundation's educational programs.

LOS ANGELES FREE CLINIC'S PROJECT ABLE—a youth theater group producing and presenting plays aimed at runaways, younger children and youth at risk. The plays deal with HIV, gangs, substance abuse, domestic violence and other issues facing kids today. In addition to education, PROJECT ABLE peers provide one-on-one counseling before and after HIV testing.

GENERAL HOSPITAL—for nearly two years, this ABC daytime television program presented a storyline abut a young man infected with AIDS and his girlfriend. The story of Robin Scorpio and Stone Cates captivated fans of *General Hospital* until the Stone character died in November 1995. Now the role of Robin continues as a young woman living with HIV. This story has taught people about AIDS and encouraged them to educate themselves about the disease and to reach out and be less afraid of those living with AIDS.

NIKKI COX—played Andrea White in the television movie *The Ryan White Story*. Now the star of Warner Brothers Network's *Unhappily Ever After*, Cox and her family have supported the work of the foundation in numerous ways.

HYATT REGENCY HOTEL INDIANAPOLIS—this hotel has been a benefactor of the Ryan White Foundation since its inception. From donating hotel rooms for foundation guests to hosting events on behalf of the foundation, the Hyatt has been one of the major contributors to the development of the foundation's programs.

ELIZABETH McAFEE—1996 "Volunteer of the Year"; an elementary school teacher. Beth unselfishly gives of her vacation time to help out at the Foundation office. Whether its's stuffing envelopes or making telephone calls, she is always ready to help. She has also served as co-chair of the Junior League's Ryan White Committee and has volunteered to work on many Foundation events.

For additional information about the work of the Ryan White Foundation, call 1-800-444-RYAN. Or write to the foundation at 1717 West 86th Street, Suite 220, Indianapolis, IN 46260.